W9-CCD-798

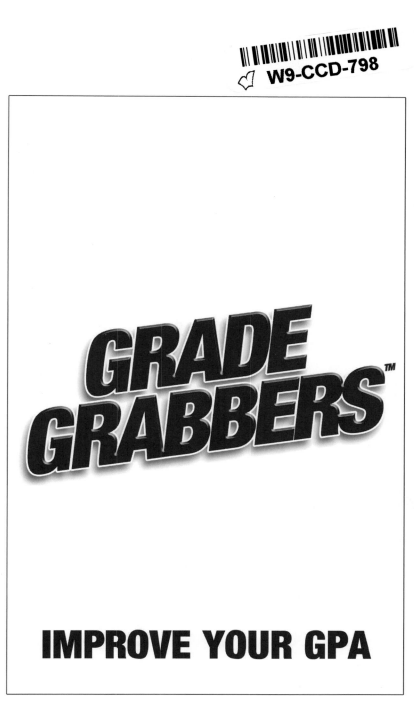

GRADE GRABBERS™

IMPROVE YOUR GPA

RICHARD MARQUIS

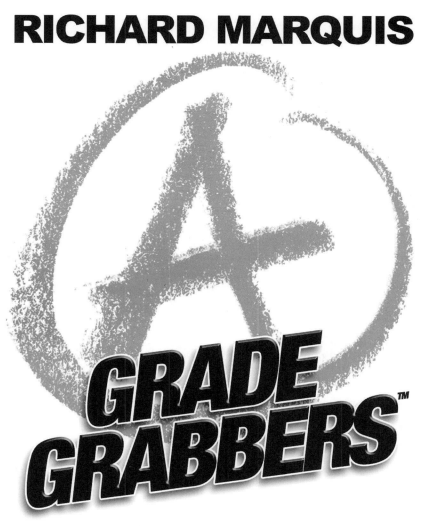

GRADE GRABBERS™

IMPROVE YOUR GPA

WRIGHT AND MEISNER PUBLISHERS, INC.
Plymouth, Michigan

Grade Grabbers: ImproveYour GPA
by Richard Marquis

Published by:
Wright and Meisner Publishers, Inc.
650 Simpson Avenue
Plymouth, MI 48170-2259 U.S.A.

orders@gradegrabbers.com
www.gradegrabbers.com

Copyright © 2006 by Richard Marquis
Printed in the United States of America

All rights reserved. No part of this book may be reproduced or transmitted in any form or by any means, electronic or mechanical, including photocopying, recording or by web distribution or by any information storage and retrieval system, without written permission from the author, except for the inclusion of brief quotations in a review.

Unattributed quotations are by Richard Marquis.
Some images by Innervision Design, Inc.
Some images by clipart.com.
Photograph of Richard Marquis by Dov Friedmann.
Cover by Innervision Design, Inc.

Library of Congress Control Number: 2005910408
ISBN-13: 978-0-9776544-0-6
ISBN-10: 0-9776544-0-0

10 9 8 7 6 5 4 3 2 1

A mon père, le grand coeur, J. Raymond Marquis

and

William Vine
A true scholar, mentor and friend

Contents

Part 8 Unlock Secrets at Your Campus Library

Part 9 Create Outasight, Outrageous, On-Target Memory Solutions (That Will Have You High-Fiving Your Friends and Your Instructors Kissing Their Grade Books!!!)

About the Author

 Richard Marquis, MA, is an award-winning scholar and researcher. He has taught Western Civilization, and American and World History at the college level. There he encountered students for whom his insightful and "to-the-point" ideas proved life changing. As an author and speaker, Richard Marquis focuses on the powerful role that quick action strategies play in making any college student more productive and successful.

Richard is no smarter than most people. He just learned to study smarter — and he couldn't be happier with the results. His name consistently appeared on the dean's list. He earned Associate and Bachelor of Arts degrees and graduated with highest honors. He served as a graduate assistant in Eastern Michigan University's Department of History. There he received a prestigious Graduate Deans' Award for Research Excellence for his Master of Arts degree thesis.

Not bad for a non-traditional student who, in his twentieth year of service on the job, was forced to leave a career in a dying industry in order to follow his dream. Was it tough at first? Sure. Was it worth it? Absolutely! Richard discovered that change brings opportunity.

Are you ready for discovery, change and opportunity? Regardless of your age or academic experience, **Richard is here to tell you, "I know you can do it!"**

If you like him as an author, you'll love him as a speaker! Are you looking for a "one-of-a-kind" keynote speaker? Is dynamic, innovative and empowering content important to you? Do you need an enthusiastically presented seminar for your campus, association or other group? **Bring Richard Marquis' "live" life-transforming message (not to mention his deep, rich voice) to your audience! Visit: www.marquisadvantage.com. E-mail: richard@marquisadvantage.com; (800) 223-2403 toll free.**

Foreword

Richard Marquis has written a simple but serious guide for the motivated college student who wishes to reach higher levels of academic achievement. The book consists of a collection of useful ideas, which are presented on single pages and are written in an easily readable, straightforward fashion. On facing pages he provides exercises designed to stimulate reflection and broaden, or strengthen, one's understanding of the particular idea being presented.

I am not aware of any other self-help book aimed at college students that has quite the character of Marquis' *Grade Grabbers*. I believe that this highly original approach to helping students attain grade improvement is likely to be most effective both because of the novel encyclopedic way the material is organized and because of the great wisdom contained in the pages' contents.

It appears that Marquis' unique perspective resulted from his own personal experience with higher education: first, his having achieved his college degrees after spending many years in the general work force; and, second, his experience as a college history teacher, a teacher who cared deeply about his students and their desire to succeed. For the student who wants to assure his or her own success in college, this little gem will certainly point the way. I especially liked those pages devoted to self-understanding and motivation, identifying and using university resources, and approaches to more efficient learning; but, the fact is, I found many treasures all through this delightful book.

Robert W. Cahill, PhD
Psychologist
Birmingham, MI
www.drrobertcahill.com

Introduction

Are you looking for surefire study ideas in a rapid-fire format that you control? Do you want to get a better handle on your college grades? Then this book is for you. *Grade Grabbers*™: *Improve Your GPA* exposes hundreds of high-impact study secrets that top students use but rarely share with their classmates.

Do you have time to waste??? Virtually every book on this subject seems to think so. *Grade Grabbers*™ is different. Just grab what you need, when you need it, and get on with your life. Isn't that what you want? If you've ever said, "Who's got time to hunt for answers?" *Grade Grabbers*™ cuts to the chase every time!

This book is for college and college-bound students and their parents, as well as nontraditional students, who want fast, effective ways to supercharge college performance. If you want to replace a slingshot approach with a guided missile, *Grade Grabbers*™ is on the launch pad, ready to go. The book you are holding will have you blasting past self-imposed barriers instantly — one page at a time! Are you ready to give it a try?

Take this three-minute challenge. Randomly open this book. Allow yourself three minutes to read both pages. If you have extra time, reread any information you wish. That's it. If you are like most students, you will be asking yourself, "Who doesn't have three minutes to become a better student?"

Grade Grabbers™ is divided into nine parts. They address the critical areas of personal motivation, organization, in-class performance, note taking and thinking skills, study tactics, working with others, test taking, research and memorization techniques. Each part contains a series of self-contained modules. Each module presents a goldmine of highly condensed, high-powered information that you can apply immediately.

Other innovative *Grade Grabbers*™ features include the headline style formatting of each topic, a variety of memory-triggering icons that will speed up the pace of your reading and review, and an innovative left-hand "Grade Grabber Exercise" page to foster the habit of asking questions prior to reading. Thought-provoking quotations round out each module. An appendix of photocopier-ready forms and a highly useful index are also provided.

Acknowledgments

This book would never have been realized without the interest, help and kindness of many people. I owe a great debt to my wife, Linda, for supporting my efforts in ways too numerous to mention. Thanks to Laurette, Joseph and Mary Marquis for generously responding to e-mails that read, "Let me know what you think of the attached...." To John, Diane, Christina and Robert Praskovich and Sarah Gruner for valuable reviews and feedback.

The late Michael Kasky, an educator who has had a lasting influence on my thinking as a student, instructor, author and professional speaker. If the reader's ultimate lesson is, "I know you can do it," this book will have been worthy of his memory.

JoAnne Lumetta, Director, Madonna University Library, for key insights on research and learning. MU's Catherine Johnstone, MA, for wise counsel. Frances FitzGerald, MA, for timely editing.

Special credit goes to Dan Poynter, CSP, publisher and owner of Para Publishing, Santa Barbara, CA. In addition to suggesting the *Grade Grabbers*™ title, his influence is seen throughout this book. NSA-Michigan for providing more support, kindness and expertise than one could imagine. Magnus Andersson of Innervision Design, Inc. is a true master who made the complicated tasks of creating the cover, website, audio CD and other designs seem simple. Michael Malenfant for his invaluable web page abilities and website management expertise.

Thanks to Doug Smart, CSP, of James & Brookfield Publishers and Leonard Charla, JD, LL, M, of Countinghouse Press, Inc. for encouragement and counsel. Terry Brock, MBA, CSP, wrote ideas about lifelong learning that were so good, I felt obliged to include them in their entirety. Dr. Bruno Cortis, MD, Fellow of the American Board of Cardiology, who speaks to the *Spiritual Heart* of his listeners. This man understands the unity of body, mind and spirit better than anyone I know. Michael Young, MS, who possesses wisdom beyond his years. Rennie Kaufmann, whose insights and contagious enthusiasm cast the project into a remarkably new light. Mat deRaad, for his valued assistance in making the soon-to-be-released *Grade Grabbers*™ audio a reality.

WARNING—DISCLAIMER

This book is designed to encourage academic success. It is sold with the understanding that the author and/or publishers are not engaged in rendering legal, health, academic advising or other professional services. If legal or other expert assistance is required, the services of a competent professional should be sought.

The specific characters and/or portrayals of such characters found in this book are fictional. The names of professors, students, mentors or anyone else used in this book's narrative or other presentations of tips, tricks or strategies serve the purpose of literary convention only. Any similarity to actual persons, living or dead, is purely coincidental.

College achievement is not automatic. Anyone who decides to attend college must expect to invest a great deal of personal time and effort without any guarantee of success. Instructors are only required to award grades which are, in their judgment, consistent with the level of learning achieved. While not all students who study are successful, all successful students study.

Every effort has been made to make this book as useful and accurate as possible. However, there may be mistakes, both typographical and in content. Therefore, this text should be used only as a general guide and not as the ultimate source of academic information.

The purpose of this book is to educate and entertain. The author and publishers cannot guarantee that using the tips, tricks, techniques and strategies contained in this book will bring successful results to anyone. The author and Wright and Meisner Publishers, Inc. shall have neither liability nor responsibility to any person or entity with respect to any loss or damage caused or alleged to be caused directly or indirectly by the information contained in this book.

If you do not wish to be bound by the above, you may return this book to the publishers for a full refund.

Part 1

Zest for Success

Grade Grabber Exercise

(QUICKLY SCAN THIS EXERCISE. JOT DOWN IDEAS, IF YOU WISH. READ THE NEXT PAGE. WRITE OR ADD TO YOUR RESPONSES BELOW. GAIN INSIGHT—TAKE ACTION!)

1. Honestly rate yourself on a scale from one to five. Your sense of mission in college could best be described as

   Adrift   1   2   3   4   5   Goal-driven

2. Is it necessary to declare a major before you can have a sense of personal mission at college? Explain.

3. What specific sorts of things are you truly passionate about? What clues might they reveal about your natural aptitudes? What do students with interests and talents similar to yours major in most?

4. Make a list of five or six of the most successful students you know. Select one or two of the most approachable classmates on your list. Ask what inspires and motivates them to succeed.

Know Why You Are in College

You are the captain
of your own destiny.
Chart your course.

Do you ever feel boxed in by
too many demands? Would you
like more control over your life, your studies and the direction in
which you are headed? Is your ability to apply expert information
and advice worth cultivating? If so, you can "reach for the stars" if
you are serious, motivated and ready to chart your course
accordingly.

Imagine the following scenario. You are a NASA astronaut
piloting your spaceship towards Mars. Not only are you millions
of miles away from the earth, but you are on this journey alone!
Yet, three important factors enable you to reach your goal.

First, you have studied and mastered your navigational maps
and itinerary. Second, your journey into space is constantly
encouraged by contact with mission control experts. Third, you
use "positive self-talk" to stay alert and focused as you meet each
challenge you encounter.

A sense of mission is just as critical for college success, even if
your academic goal is yet to be discovered. It begins with attitude.
You can greatly increase your chances of succeeding the way
many top students do, if you keep the following in mind:

1. Anything worth doing is worth doing in and of itself.
   It can inspire your study, mastery and success.
2. You are entitled to academic "mission control" help.
   Instructors, counselors, research librarians and the
   like are prepared to offer you expert advice.
3. Positive self-talk promotes goal-centered attitudes.
   A student on a mission is able to ask, "Why not?"

"LIFE GOES ON; I FORGET JUST WHY."
— EDNA ST. VINCENT MILLAY

Grade Grabber Exercise

(QUICKLY SCAN THIS EXERCISE. JOT DOWN IDEAS, IF
YOU WISH. READ THE NEXT PAGE. WRITE OR ADD TO
YOUR RESPONSES BELOW. GAIN INSIGHT—TAKE ACTION!)

1. How important is a sense of self-worth in pursuing academic
   success? Is it inborn? Can it be learned? Explain.

2. Have you ever used the power of visualization to succeed in
   sports or some other skill-related endeavor? Provide one or two
   examples of this.

3. In what way can you make your future academic success
   tangible—something you can physically pick up and examine?

4. Although a "Positive Foregone Conclusion" represents a
   successful outcome, is it also possible for you to enjoy the
   journey towards its realization? Give an example of how this is
   or is not possible.

Trust in Your Ability to Learn and to Realize Your Goals

Dynamically visualize "Positive Foregone Conclusions" to focus and empower your mind and your performance.

"Positive Foregone Conclusions" and the commitment to trust in and to pursue your passion is a powerful way to accelerate learning. Many, many traditional and nontraditional students can vouch for the validity of this approach. The great news is that it can work for you. All you need is a clear goal, the necessary motivation to reach that goal and the openness to change your life—for the better.

Something astounding happens when you invoke PFC in connection with a worthwhile goal. Your objective does not seem quite so distant after all. At times, you intuitively feel that you could almost reach out and touch it. You discover that the world in general, as well as the world of academe, becomes transformed.

Life becomes more of an adventure. The principle of "Positive Foregone Conclusions" has the power to give you hope, healthy self-worth and a clear sense of mission, regardless of whether your goal is modest or monumental. Putting this process to work for you is a snap.

Make it visual. Picture yourself successfully making an oral presentation in class. **Make it tangible.** Sense the temperature in the room. Feel your hands touching the podium. **Make it audible.** Hear yourself speaking with clarity and confidence to a roomful of interested classmates. Hear your instructor saying, "Well done!" as you end your presentation. **Make it fun.** Why not imagine yourself thoroughly enjoying the experience?

Now there is a "Positive Foregone Conclusion!"

"IF YOU THINK YOU CAN, YOU CAN. IF YOU THINK YOU CAN'T, YOU CAN'T. EITHER WAY, YOU ARE RIGHT." —HENRY FORD

Grade Grabber Exercise

(QUICKLY SCAN THIS EXERCISE. JOT DOWN IDEAS, IF
YOU WISH. READ THE NEXT PAGE. WRITE OR ADD TO
YOUR RESPONSES BELOW. GAIN INSIGHT—TAKE ACTION!)

1. An arbitrary attitude often destroys otherwise promising work.
   What do top students do to keep their work on track?

2. How can being more humane with yourself encourage your
   thinking ability?

3. What sorts of characteristics are present when you are at your
   "level worst"? Have you ever noticed what might trigger them?
   (Example: Inadequate rest.)

4. What sorts of characteristics are present when you are at your
   level best?

Cultivate Your Aptitude for Patience

Being more humane with yourself can transform your approach to learning.

You have, no doubt, heard the proverb, "Patience is its own reward." Now, be honest. How patient are you with yourself? We live in demanding times. So do not feel bad if you are frequently hard on yourself. Family, work and academic demands can burden any student with worry and stress.

But you can be attentive and resourceful in stressful times by watching for signs of obsessive worry. Cultivating patience is a precious skill that most anyone can develop. Patience is not simply a rite of passage. It reinforces your trust in yourself and in your ability to think on your feet and to learn—no matter what demands are swirling around you.

Realize this valuable insight: When arbitrariness replaces logic, it is almost always the first step towards obsessiveness and worry.

Trust yourself. Be patient with yourself. Be kind to yourself. You can transform your approach to learning. Note the following:

PATIENT TRUST	OBSESSIVE WORRY
1. Logical	1. Arbitrary
2. Vigilant	2. Agitated
3. Optimistic	3. Dreading
4. Self-forgiving	4. Self-loathing
5. Appreciative	5. Thankless
6. Self-directed	6. Driven
7. Seeks discovery	7. Seeks conquest
8. Is its own reward	8. Is its own punishment
9. Expansive	9. Destructive

"GENIUS IS ONLY A GREATER APTITUDE FOR PATIENCE."
—GEORGES-LOUIS LECLERC DE BUFFON

Grade Grabber Exercise

(QUICKLY SCAN THIS EXERCISE. JOT DOWN IDEAS, IF
YOU WISH. READ THE NEXT PAGE. WRITE OR ADD TO
YOUR RESPONSES BELOW. GAIN INSIGHT—TAKE ACTION!)

1. How important a role can self-esteem play in academic success?

2. How is having a healthy sense of self-worth different from being "stuck on oneself"? Explain.

3. Describe a simple method for developing self-esteem. Is there a fast track to attaining it?

4. Does high self-esteem mean that you will value others less than you do now? Explain. What is the most empowering benefit of a healthy self-image?

See a Top Student's Face in the Mirror

A five-second pep talk can help you draw on powerful inner resources.

First impressions are lasting impressions. Realize that your academic image is important. How do you see yourself? Whatever your answer, it should be clear that healthy self-esteem is a vital part of the process. After all, how can you hope to positively impress others if you do not value your own worth? But do not forget that you must value others, as well.

Healthy self-esteem seeks to balance an authentic, humane and supportive sense of your own value. This enables you to encourage the best traits in others, too. **Narcissism**, on the other hand, is an unhealthy, ruthless and annoying form of self-infatuation. It manipulates and excludes others. Avoid it.

Cultivating a healthy self-esteem can revolutionize your outlook and expand your learning potential, as well as your ability to work with others. Although it requires effort, your academic self-image and ongoing success can be developed. You can do this as you begin each day. Many top students do. Simply use the last few seconds in front of the bathroom mirror for a quick pep talk.

1. "See" yourself as loyal and trustworthy. Send yourself simple and direct acceptance and encouragement.
2. Once that "registers," take five seconds to hold on to your self-validating image. With practice, you can recall your success image as clearly as if you had sketched it out.
3. Say the words, "Let's go get 'em!" and begin your day.

Self-acceptance truly empowers you. And, your self-acceptance can positively influence and empower others with whom you come into contact in mutually helpful and healthful ways. Do it.

All it takes is a few seconds: See the picture. Say the words.

"TO ACCEPT OURSELVES AS WE ARE MEANS TO VALUE OUR IMPERFECTIONS AS MUCH AS OUR PERFECTIONS." —SANDRA BIERIG

Grade Grabber Exercise

(QUICKLY SCAN THIS EXERCISE. JOT DOWN IDEAS, IF
YOU WISH. READ THE NEXT PAGE. WRITE OR ADD TO
YOUR RESPONSES BELOW. GAIN INSIGHT—TAKE ACTION!)

1. What one image best symbolizes personal excellence for you?

2. Although information overload is common today, think up
    two or three ideas that can help you to better control it.

3. Who in your life most resists change? What are their results?

4. In what ways are you responsible for your own learning
    outside of an academic setting? Give one or two examples.

Learn for the Long Run

Lay your foundation for learning excellence, one stride at a time.

Twenty-six centuries ago, the first "marathon runner" ran twenty-six miles to report astonishing information in Athens. Greece won the Battle of Marathon at a loss of 192 lives, compared to 6,400 Persians killed. To this day, the image of the marathon runner remains one of the most compelling symbols of personal excellence and endurance imaginable.

Modern psychologists would generally agree that the power of this ancient story of victory against unthinkable odds comes from its universal quality, unbounded by time or space.

Today you are an active participant in an exciting, although stressful, turning point in human history. It is a time in which information frequently seems to invade and overrun every corner of daily life. What might you do to transform this stumbling block into your own foundation and cornerstone for future success? Commit yourself to a life of unending learning and growth!

Realize that non-stop learners have become the new marathoners. Just as you can find examples of long-distance runners, you can do the same thing to become a lifelong learner. Look for them and then look to them for your example. They can both inspire and challenge you to continually push your present limits and abilities, step by step, like any good marathoner does.

Every important journey begins with the first step. But you must keep your ears alert to the cadence of today's informational marathoners. Begin your quest to become more. You are not alone.

"SCHOOL CONTINUES NON-STOP FOR TODAY'S PROFESSIONAL. ONCE YOU'RE FREE OF THE GRIND OF TESTS AND WHAT YOU HAVE TO DO, YOU GET TO PUT YOURSELF INTO YOUR OWN 'UNIVERSITY OF YOU' AND LEARN THOSE THINGS THAT ARE MOST IMPORTANT TO YOU. YOU ARE THE PROFESSOR. YOU ARE THE STUDENT. ALL SUCCESSFUL PEOPLE MUST ATTEND THIS UNIVERSITY REGARDLESS OF WHERE THEY GOT THEIR FORMAL EDUCATION." —TERRY BROCK

Grade Grabber Exercise

(QUICKLY SCAN THIS EXERCISE. JOT DOWN IDEAS, IF YOU WISH. READ THE NEXT PAGE. WRITE OR ADD TO YOUR RESPONSES BELOW. GAIN INSIGHT—TAKE ACTION!)

1. Honestly rate yourself on a scale from one to five. How much of a perfectionist are you, usually?

   Laid back   1   2   3   4   5   Unbending

2. Honestly rate yourself on a scale from one to five. How much of a perfectionist do you become when stressed out?

   Laid back   1   2   3   4   5   Unbending

3. Honestly rate yourself on a scale from one to five. How often do you appreciate the many gifts that daily life offers you?

   Never   1   2   3   4   5   Often

4. Add your own ideas to the following list of things for which many people are thankful: Family, friends, a favorite pet, health, food, laughter, kindness, music, sports, movies, etc.

5. What ten-minute activity could make your daily life more enjoyable? Watch truly "happy" people in your life for clues.

Lighten Up On Yourself

Be kind to your mind. Both you and
your brain need a break, now and then.

Academic achievement is a work in
progress. Regardless of your goals, you need to
cultivate time and patience with yourself. You
may have scheduled your classes sensibly. You may have wisely
distributed the demands of study, work, rest and recreation. But
you need to be sure that you keep them in balance. Like any well-
laid plan, it is always possible to backslide.

Although laziness can be a problem, it is highly unlikely that a
lazy student would be reading this book. Your greatest danger is
at the opposite end of the spectrum.

Demanding a reasonable level of personal exertion is one
thing. Overtaxing yourself is quite another. You need to steer clear
of an abusive approach to your academic goals. When you
abandon your physical and emotional needs for rest, nutrition and
recreation, you risk doing great harm to yourself.

To counter that deadly trap, strive to invest yourself in those
things that keep you energized, happy, strong and resilient.
Consider the following tips to keep your academic life in balance:

- Dim lights and avoid caffeine three hours before bedtime.
- Get the sleep you need on a regular basis.
- Include a daily walk or other exercise and stick with it.
- Reserve a specific time for rest, leisure and recreation.
- Practice meditation, stretching or breathing exercises.
- Eat healthy foods and take vitamin supplements.
- Enjoy leisurely breaks with others.
- Quickly reenergize yourself with ten-minute catnaps.
- Let your inner child occasionally direct your behavior.
- Rest your brain by watching a cartoon with a storyline
  that "always" makes you laugh (example: *Road Runner*).

"PEOPLE WHO CANNOT FIND TIME FOR RECREATION ARE OBLIGED,
SOONER OR LATER, TO FIND TIME FOR ILLNESS." —JOHN WANAMAKER

Grade Grabber Exercise

(QUICKLY SCAN THIS EXERCISE. JOT DOWN IDEAS, IF YOU WISH. READ THE NEXT PAGE. WRITE OR ADD TO YOUR RESPONSES BELOW. GAIN INSIGHT—TAKE ACTION!)

1. List five ways in which your campus cafeteria can be your oasis and help you to develop your potential for future success.

2. How might studying with friends in a cafeteria be superior to studying with them in a private room at the library?

3. All students need time to study alone. How might taking a break to "just be" with people renew your focus and stamina during prolonged and solitary work? Explain.

Enter Your Oasis

Re-energizing your brain, body and spirit can be as simple as a visit to the cafeteria.

Virtually every campus has a cafeteria or snack bar to which students naturally gravitate. Your campus is probably one of them. If you look at such an area as an oasis made just for you—and every student should feel that way—it can be a place of comfort, pause and renewal. And who could possibly be against that?

Socializing with colleagues is important for lifelong success and well being. So, too, is the ability to work independently. Yet, even when working hard to earn top grades, break time is critical.

One of the many healthful aspects of campus life is that it offers facilities that can renew you personally, as well as intellectually. Consider how maximizing your use of a campus cafeteria can transform your most challenging desert of discontent into a life-giving oasis:

1. Renewing old acquaintances with
   a. Fellow students.
   b. Instructors.
   c. Library staff.
   d. Counselors.
2. Making new acquaintances
   a. By chance.
   b. By personal introduction.
   c. By being introduced through others.
3. Taking time by yourself to
   a. Neutralize normal feelings of isolation.
   b. Reconnect and just "be" in the moment.
   c. Positively address hunger or fatigue.
   d. Be kind to your mind.

"NOW AND THEN IT'S GOOD TO PAUSE IN OUR PURSUIT OF HAPPINESS AND JUST BE HAPPY." —GUILLAUME APPOLINAIRE

Part 2

Don't Let an Hourglass Kick Sand in Your Face!

Grade Grabber Exercise

(QUICKLY SCAN THIS EXERCISE. JOT DOWN IDEAS, IF
YOU WISH. READ THE NEXT PAGE. WRITE OR ADD TO
YOUR RESPONSES BELOW. GAIN INSIGHT—TAKE ACTION!)

1. What sorts of things do you tend to postpone most?

2. What words best describe your justification for postponing important work? Jot down two or three responses.

3. Rationalization occurs every time that we invent "good" reasons to make objectively harmful decisions. Be honest. How often do your responses to #2 stem from rationalization?

   Never   1   2   3   4   5   Always

4. Name one task that you have you been putting off. How might taking immediate, positive action create a happier outcome?

Flash Past Road Blocks to Success

Make an action decision right now! Each positive stride liberates you from self-imposed limits.

Have you ever put off something unpleasant? Have you ever lived to regret the nightmare that decision caused you? Would you like to reduce your stress and increase the quality of your academic work as so many top students do? If so, identifying the source and consequences of procrastination and rededicating yourself to renewed initiative can spell success.

Rescheduling due to an emergency, crisis or loss is one thing. Procrastination is entirely another. Mediocre students often rationalize their delays by "spinning" excuses for putting off tasks they find distasteful. "What harm can it do?"

While such decisions often bring some initial relief, the effects do not last long. Frequently, more excuses and more delays pile up until deadlines loom so large that these students find themselves caught in a trap of their own making. Stress, confusion and low quality work become almost unavoidable as student resilience crumbles.

Think about it. Procrastination can lead to and/or aggravate:

- Fearfulness
- Anxiety
- Low Self-Esteem
- Dread
- Panic
- Depression
- Hopelessness
- Destructiveness

Yet, decisive energetic strides can clear your way to success.

"YOU CAN ONLY DECIDE HOW YOU'RE GOING TO LIVE NOW."
—JOAN BAEZ

Grade Grabber Exercise

(QUICKLY SCAN THIS EXERCISE. JOT DOWN IDEAS, IF YOU WISH. READ THE NEXT PAGE. WRITE OR ADD TO YOUR RESPONSES BELOW. GAIN INSIGHT—TAKE ACTION!)

1. What is your most unrealistic approach to time management?

2. Do you occasionally schedule time to review your workload? Explain.

3. In what ways do you keep your semester projects and deadlines on track? What usually causes you to lose track?

4. Is it possible to "have it all" by always refusing to put limits on yourself? Give examples from personal experience.

Plan Your Time Realistically

You can avoid burnout by conserving your most valuable resources.

Our modern "supersized" culture has convinced many people that they "can have it all!" But the reality is that nobody can. Each of us must draw from limited personal reserves of time, energy and talent in order to accomplish any worthwhile goal, scholastic or otherwise.

Think about it this way: Until the day comes when you can "supersize" your calendar from its current one-pound capacity, you can't expect to pour two pounds of life into it.

Ignore this fact and you will end up being your own worst enemy, even if you don't burn yourself out in the process.

Consider these four key factors to help prevent burnout:

1. Use feedback.
2. Target effectively.
3. Respectfully care for yourself.
4. Work your plan.

First, realize that false ambition speculates; true ambition calculates. Use feedback from friends, family and advisers, and the syllabus and calendar to help you keep your goals on track and in balance. Second, know your target. Be specific about the amount of study and time needed to earn the kind of grades you are targeting. Third, maintain healthy levels of rest, recreational and nutritional resources, and respect the fact that they are not limitless. Finally, execute around the goals or mission statement that you have thoughtfully put together, and associate with those who will support you in making your reasonable plan a reality. Reason is the only "all" you really need.

"ACCEPT, RESPECT AND APPRECIATE YOURSELF."
—BRUNO CORTIS, MD

MY DAILY AGENDA

DATE-

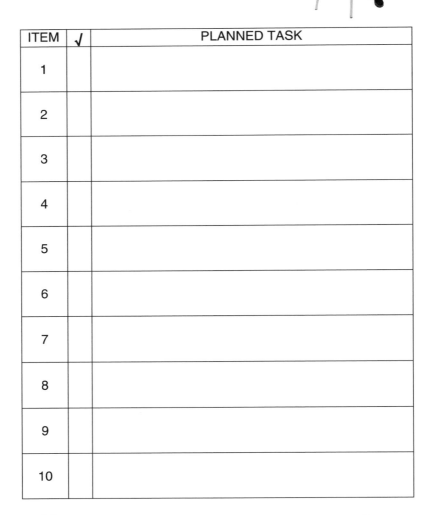

ITEM	√	PLANNED TASK
1		
2		
3		
4		
5		
6		
7		
8		
9		
10		

"GOALS THAT ARE NOT WRITTEN DOWN ARE JUST WISHES."
—ANONYMOUS

Plan Your Day

Putting daily goals in writing can help you surpass them, while encouraging balance.

It is great to end the day just as you had planned it, especially when important goals are successfully met. Top students regularly experience this feeling. Yet, their mediocre classmates frequently leave too much undone. If you want to use your time more efficiently, include those items in your daily agenda that will pay the greatest return for your time and effort.

Should you include weekly and monthly agenda targets? Of course. All students should. Yet, many poor students fail to consider the importance of establishing critical, personal, daily goals. Why imitate failure? Target and then focus your attention. Prioritize and master critical course areas. Realize real, measurable progress in your efforts, one day at a time. It is simple.

Begin each day by targeting ten important and achievable goals. Make certain that each goal in your agenda represents a worthwhile academic purpose or directly contributes to it. **Create and/or use a standardized form for this task. Write your daily agenda. Your sense of organization, direction and purpose will increase as you complete each agenda item.**

In formulating your day's agenda, choose goals that are:

1. Reasonable in scope. Balance individual class demands.
2. Realizable within the time limits available to you.
3. Really worthy of your time.

Choosing to tackle whatever happens to come along is not a plan. It is a reaction. Prioritizing sharpens judgment. Some tasks are important. Some are not. A little forethought, combined with small steps, can produce much more consistent academic work. Consider your needs. Plan your agenda. Work your plan. Achieve.

"DON'T WORRY IF YOU DON'T COMPLETE EVERYTHING ON THE SCHEDULE. AT LEAST YOU WILL HAVE COMPLETED THE MOST IMPORTANT PROJECTS BEFORE GETTING TO THE LESS IMPORTANT ONES." —IVY LEE

QUARTER HOUR STUDY POWER

DATE-
SUBJECT-
TEXT-

(Use this form* with the instructions on the opposite page. Feel free to substitute graph paper if you wish. Do what works best!)

TIME: START TO FINISH	15	30	45	00	ACTUAL HOURLY STUDY TIME	ACTUAL HOURLY PAGES READ	ASSIGNED PAGES: 37
3:00 pm	√ 3	-	√ 4	√ 4	3/4	11	26
4:00 pm	√ 3	√ 5	√ 4	√ 3	1	15	11
5:00 pm	√ 2	-	-	-	1/4	2	9
					TOTAL STUDY TIME	TOTAL PAGES READ	ASSIGNED PAGES REMAINING
					2 HRS.	28 PAGES	9 PAGES

*Photocopier-ready forms are available in the Appendix.

Learn the Power of the Quarter Hour

Natural pacing instantly controls time, content and stress.

How would you like to maintain higher, more consistent levels of energy as you study? Many top students do. They use fifteen-minute study intervals to stimulate positive, measurable results. Why not put them to work for you?

After selecting a subject for study, take out a sheet of standard lined or graph paper to use as a timesheet. Before beginning, assess your needs. Establish how many pages you have to read, study or review and how much time there is available to you. Set a timer for a series of fifteen-minute sessions and begin your work.

Some students put a check mark on their time sheets. Many top students record each quarter hour of work by noting the number of pages completed. Either way, focus, control and natural pacing:

- Instantly reveal how efficiently you use time.
- Outline your time requirements by subject.
- Reward your progress with objective feedback.
- Flag problems before they can affect your grades.
- Promote focus by limiting your attention to task, time and targets.
- Make it easier to break off and/or resume study.
- Help you to better serve yourself and to stay on task longer.
- Eventually stimulate hours of progress that can deepen your inner sense of direction and purpose!
- Provide you with accurate documentation to review with your instructor or colleagues.
- Promote personal accountability, regardless of circumstances, while conserving time and energy.

"QUIET MINDS CAN'T BE PERPLEXED OR FRIGHTENED, BUT GO ON IN FORTUNE OR MISFORTUNE AT THEIR OWN PRIVATE PACE, LIKE A CLOCK DURING A THUNDERSTORM." —ROBERT LOUIS STEVENSON

Grade Grabber Exercise

(QUICKLY SCAN THIS EXERCISE. JOT DOWN IDEAS, IF
YOU WISH. READ THE NEXT PAGE. WRITE OR ADD TO
YOUR RESPONSES BELOW. GAIN INSIGHT—TAKE ACTION!)

1. Picture yourself arriving at class on the day an important
   written assignment is due—and it is missing! What is your
   normal response? Explain.

2. What is the worst last-minute crisis that you have ever
   observed in another student? Use three or four words to
   describe what it taught you.

3. Take 30-45 seconds to list as many "deadline" emergencies
   as you can. Discuss your list with a sharp classmate on break.

4. From the Instructors As People Department: Ask instructors
   to recall their biggest "deadline" nightmares. Listen for sharp,
   practical and often humorous insights.

Prepare for the Unthinkable

Power failures and other last-minute emergencies can sabotage the best-laid plans.

You are making that "final, final" semester draft. You warily eye the clock as it ticks down to "zero" hour. You think, "Now if nothing goes wrong, I can just make my deadline."

And then, "Presto!" As if by magic, you are hit by a power outage. All of your data is on the hard drive, of course. Frantically, you call every person you know within a close radius to you. Some are home. Some are not. None can help.

Chances are that, sometime during your college years, you will experience at least one huge beast of a crisis that will fray your nerves and try your patience. Consider the following:

- Regularly back up work to a USB flash drive, CD, etc.
- Add an "ICE" (In Case of Emergency) contact number to your cell phone book. Not only does this inform medical personnel in an emergency, but it also increases your chances of getting your cell phone back if you lose it!
- Keep a duplicate car key in your wallet. If you are ever locked out of your car, you will be glad to have it.
- E-mail a file copy to Yahoo!© mail, MSN© Hotmail™ or a similar web-accessible account. They are free and reliable.
- Use plastic folders to protect paperwork from the rain.
- Carry an emergency backup copy of your paper.
- Carry a stapler and a staple puller for redoing pages.
- Plant seeds of good will before a crisis hits. Many students do the opposite and are upset when they meet resistance.
- Immediately call your instructor about any emergency.
- Envision your worst-case scenario and take steps to prevent it from happening, but do not obsess over it.
- Back off of yourself. Everyone has bad days.

"DEEP DESPAIR AWAITS THE UNPREPARED." —MARC SCHOENBERG

Grade Grabber Exercise
(QUICKLY SCAN THIS EXERCISE. JOT DOWN IDEAS, IF YOU WISH. READ THE NEXT PAGE. WRITE OR ADD TO YOUR RESPONSES BELOW. GAIN INSIGHT—TAKE ACTION!)

1. In which classes do you need to bring supplies that are different from those used in most other subjects?

2. Take a moment to organize a list of crucial supplies. Especially notice those items that you run out of most or are often "sold out" during exam time. How could you avoid future problems?

ESSENTIAL SUPPLIES		

Pack Plenty of Routine Supplies

A lack of necessities can jeopardize your grades.

Professor Davis cannot believe his ears when Robin asks him for a blank blue book. After all, the final exam of the semester is already underway. The clock is ticking. "Sorry," he says. "That is your responsibility, not mine."

Robin asks her classmates, but none of them has an extra blue book to give her. They are too busy writing their exam responses to worry about her problem. As Robin slips out of the classroom and feverishly runs to the bookstore, her panic increases. She wonders if she will have enough time to complete her exam.

Successful students strive to avoid such a crisis by having enough supplies for all of their classes. Do you want to succeed?

Here is a list of the most commonly used supplies that you will need.

ROUTINE SUPPLIES		
Syllabus (Updated?)	Calculator	Highlighter pens
Course handouts	**Writing tablet**	Ruler
Texts and Notes	**Scantron© or other scannable test form**	Glue stick
Pens (black)	**Blue Book**	Paper clips
Pencils (No. 2) --pre-sharpened	Stapler (small) with standard-size refills	Adhesive tape
Sharpener (pocket)	Staple puller	Sticky notes
Eraser ("gum" type)	**Liquid correction fluid**	Note cards: 5"x 8"

How prepared are you to earn the best grades possible?

"THE DOGS MAY BARK BUT THE CARAVAN MOVES ON."
—ARABIC PROVERB

Part 3
Top Student or Flop Student?

Grade Grabber Exercise

(QUICKLY SCAN THIS EXERCISE. JOT DOWN IDEAS, IF YOU WISH. READ THE NEXT PAGE. WRITE OR ADD TO YOUR RESPONSES BELOW. GAIN INSIGHT—TAKE ACTION!)

1. Imagine that you are a college professor. What specific qualities would you look for in your best students?

2. Continuing in your role as college professor, what sorts of challenges and benefits might you expect from better students?

3. Honestly rate yourself on a scale from one to five. Generally speaking, how prepared are you for in-class instructor questions?

   Never   1   2   3   4   5   Always

4. Regardless of how you rated yourself, you get a second chance. What are you prepared to do to create positive change and/or maximize your instructor's opinion of you as a serious student?

12 Ways to Positively Impress Your Instructor

Giving them what they want, and...

The football coaching legend, Vince Lombardi, was asked if there was one word that best summarized his ability to succeed. His answer came without the slightest hesitation: "KISS--Keep it simple, stupid!"

Do you want to succeed in your studies? Then make it a point to do whatever work your instructor requires. Simply do the work, regardless of how little or how much you like the subject.

Here are twelve ways to impress virtually any instructor, while making any class that you take more enriching and enjoyable.

1. Introduce yourself to your instructor on day one.
2. Ask questions whenever you need clarification.
3. Meet with your instructor to review your progress.
4. Be conscientious about appointments and deadlines.
5. Keep non-academic problems and concerns to yourself.
6. Consider all extra credit work as mandatory assignments.
7. Respect and support the rights of others to their opinions.
8. Build trust: Communicate, communicate, communicate.
9. Be familiar with and regularly refer to your syllabus.
10. Study and prepare for all in-class responses and sharing.
11. Work as though what you are doing is important. It is.
12. Be willing to be open, to be corrected and to grow.

Remember Vince Lombardi's advice and take action today. Just as in sports, academic success requires a reliable game plan.

Don't kiss it off.

"THE SUCCESSFUL PERSON IS THE INDIVIDUAL WHO FORMS THE HABIT OF DOING WHAT THE FAILING PERSON DOESN'T LIKE TO DO."
—DONALD RIGGS

Grade Grabber Exercise

(QUICKLY SCAN THIS EXERCISE. JOT DOWN IDEAS, IF
YOU WISH. READ THE NEXT PAGE. WRITE OR ADD TO
YOUR RESPONSES BELOW. GAIN INSIGHT—TAKE ACTION!)

1. Should you feel obligated to sit near a friend if he insists on disrupting in-class lectures? Explain.

2. How do you react when someone is talking, laughing, etc. during lectures or in-class presentations? Why would good students share or not share your point of view?

3. Recall a case of self-sabotage that resulted in a lower grade for a student you know. What lesson did it teach you?

10 Ways to Cut Your Own Throat in Class

Who awards your grades, anyway?

Your professors can ultimately make or break your grade point average. Yet your attitude will always be the biggest factor in that process. "Knowledge is power." Know it!!! Your value to an instructor quickly skyrockets if you are an asset to yourself, your instructor and your classmates. "Assets pay dividends." Think payday!

Oddly, many students behave as though they do not need to be on good terms with instructors. Although actually guilty of self-sabotage, they usually attempt to save face by blaming their instructors, rather than themselves. What is worse, they frequently undercut fellow classmates while virtually guaranteeing their own failure. Here is a list of ways to compromise your GPA:

1. Arrive late and/or leave early without prior agreement.
2. Do not take notes or take part in class discussions.
3. Ask questions that reveal ignorance of assigned reading.
4. Formulate questions with little or no relevance to class.
5. Submit incomplete, unauthorized or late assignments.
6. Refuse to provide requested documentation for absences.
7. Question your instructor's integrity for simply using the same standards with you that are used with others.
8. Bring food into class; fall asleep in class; get awakened by the instructor — of the next class.
9. Bring friends into class and/or chitchat during class.
10. Assume that the instructor must be available 24/7 for a make-up test or exam; later on, attempt to **re**-reschedule it.

The moral? Be reasonable. Be focused. Go out of your way to be an asset, not a liability. Payment of tuition only enrolls you in a class for the semester; it does not entitle you to a passing grade.

"A MAN WRAPPED UP IN HIMSELF MAKES A VERY SMALL BUNDLE."
—BENJAMIN FRANKLIN

Grade Grabber Exercise

(QUICKLY SCAN THIS EXERCISE. JOT DOWN IDEAS, IF
YOU WISH. READ THE NEXT PAGE. WRITE OR ADD TO
YOUR RESPONSES BELOW. GAIN INSIGHT—TAKE ACTION!)

1. How reliable have you found student recommendations
   regarding professors and classes? Give one or two examples.

2. List six to eight reasons for selecting a particular professor
   and/or class.

3. What are some red flags to look out for in an instructor?

4. How might you decide whether you should drop a class or not?
   How quickly should you drop a class?

Know When to Drop a Class

Trust your gut when it comes to instructors.

You have just started your new semester. It has been a week or so since you began your classes. But one particular class has been nagging at the pit of your stomach from day one, in a way that no other class has managed to do. It has gotten so bad that you are seriously considering dropping a class for the first time since you decided to get a degree.

Perhaps you signed up for it on a blind hunch. Maybe your decision was based on a recommendation you received from an anonymous student, while standing in line to register. Rethink it.

While there may be times when a variety of demands force you to sign up for a class taught by a less-than-desirable instructor, strive to keep your options open.

Even if you normally "hang tough," you should consider a few factors that might justify dropping an instructor's class:

- Speech mannerisms that make note taking very difficult.
- Gives directions that are unclear or confusing to you.
- Refuses to slow down when asked.
- Refuses to answer questions.
- Refuses to give an "A" grade—to anyone.
- Likes to flunk the entire class on the first test.
- Workload undermines or jeopardizes your other courses.
- Refuses to offer a reasonable office hour schedule.
- Lacks common courtesy and/or permits the same.
- Refuses to take your concerns seriously.

Head off disaster. Trust your gut when it comes to instructors. If you think you should drop a class, you probably should.

"I NEVER SAW A WRECK AND NEVER HAVE BEEN WRECKED NOR WAS I EVER IN ANY PREDICAMENT THAT THREATENED TO END IN DISASTER OF ANY SORT." —E.J. SMITH, CAPTAIN, HMS TITANIC

Grade Grabber Exercise

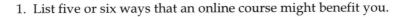

(QUICKLY SCAN THIS EXERCISE. JOT DOWN IDEAS, IF YOU WISH. READ THE NEXT PAGE. WRITE OR ADD TO YOUR RESPONSES BELOW. GAIN INSIGHT—TAKE ACTION!)

1. List five or six ways that an online course might benefit you.

2. List five or six ways that an online course might not be your best option.

3. In what ways does an online course change the dynamics of your interaction with instructors and fellow students?

4. In what ways is an academic chat room different from conventional internet chat rooms? Why is this difference important to keep in mind?

Consider Online Courses

Distance learning may be just right for you.

Technology has caused a revolution in the academic world. More and more online courses are offered in response to the demands of increasingly busy and computer-savvy students. Yet, online class rolls often experience a higher student withdrawal rate than their conventional semester counterparts. Quite often such "drops" result from naïve student assumptions when registering for an online class. Smart students work within their strengths. They consider and then select the right course for them.

Is an online course best for you? Carefully consider your own learning approach. Compare it with that of the most successful online distance learners. There is no need to be fatalistic. At times, slight adjustments can vastly improve your performance. Be realistic. Sometimes it is better to consider other course options.

The following list is not exhaustive. But it does provide an accurate overview of traits that instructors commonly observe in their top-performing online students. These traits include:

- Strong organizational and course-preparation habits.
- Solid college-level writing skills.
- Computer savvy.
- Flexibility with regard to power, technical or software-related failure, such as during online tests, etc.
- Chat room courtesy towards instructors and fellow students. (Their motto: "'Flaming' only burns you!")
- Doing without the usual visual and/or verbal stimulation, interaction and feedback associated with classrooms.
- Filtering out distractions at work or at home.
- Working alone without feeling "isolated."
- Personal motivation, accountability and productivity.

"MOTIVATION IS SIMPLE. YOU ELIMINATE THOSE WHO ARE NOT MOTIVATED." –LOU HOLTZ

Grade Grabber Exercise

(QUICKLY SCAN THIS EXERCISE. JOT DOWN IDEAS, IF
YOU WISH. READ THE NEXT PAGE. WRITE OR ADD TO
YOUR RESPONSES BELOW. GAIN INSIGHT—TAKE ACTION!)

1. What is the ultimate purpose for awarding a football (or other) scholarship?

2. Are such scholarships "fireproof," or do athletes have to maintain passing grades?

3. Do star football players deserve special treatment if they have had a winning season, yet have failed academically? Explain.

4. What is the best piece of advice that someone on an athletic scholarship might keep in mind at college?

Balance Study and Sports, and Your Scholarship Will Take Care of Itself

Athletic success alone cannot carry you across the academic goal line.

Imagine this scene. Dr. JoAnne Johnson presses the "enter" button on her computer, sending her final batch of grades to academic records, closing out another academic year.

"It's over," she thinks to herself. Sporadic shouts from students can be heard as they make their last trips to the dorm.

Suddenly, Mike, a burly 6'3" fullback, emerges from the noisy hallway and enters the professor's office. Tearfully, he collapses into the nearest chair, protesting the reality swirling around him. "If I don't get at least a 'C,' I'm going to lose my scholarship!"

"You haven't worked all semester, Mike. You deserve an 'E.' Period. By the way, I don't appreciate your trying to get the coach to bail you out again. In fact, both of us have had it with your failure to keep the tutoring appointments we set up. He made it a point to inform me that all of your teammates have studied hard and done well. So you see, Mike . . . "

"But if you don't give me a better grade, I'll not only flunk this class, I'll lose my football scholarship! Can't you give me some extra credit work to do? There's still time, isn't there?"

As the rumbling sound of moving vans interrupts the conversation, an icy realization echoes in the young man's brain. "I can't afford to go to college. Now what do I do?"

"Perhaps you can come back later, when you've earned the money. Didn't you tell me that your brother just won a scholarship? It's too late for you, but knowing your story might challenge him to take his studies more seriously."

"HOW BITTER A THING TO LOOK INTO HAPPINESS THROUGH ANOTHER MAN'S EYES." —WILLIAM SHAKESPEARE

Grade Grabber Exercise

(QUICKLY SCAN THIS EXERCISE. JOT DOWN IDEAS, IF YOU WISH. READ THE NEXT PAGE. WRITE OR ADD TO YOUR RESPONSES BELOW. GAIN INSIGHT—TAKE ACTION!)

1. When are you most inclined to speak with your instructors? Do you normally try to avoid them as much as possible? Explain.

2. What are the most common reasons mediocre students give for speaking with an instructor?

3. How can taking the initiative to speak with an instructor give you a distinct advantage, even though you are new to college?

4. Imagine a conversation with your instructor in which you learn her subject area of interest. How might this help you to study more effectively for her class? Explain.

Value Your Instructor's Expertise

If you will only step forward and ask, your instructor can listen and provide helpful suggestions.

This scene is almost certainly played out in a good number of classrooms on most, if not all, college campuses. The instructor has just completed her day's lecture and pauses after collecting a few last items to take with her. Although she is attentive, alert and willing to go the extra mile with her students, she is preoccupied for the moment. Her thoughts have turned to a mandatory departmental meeting scheduled for 2:00 p.m. She has an hour to kill. Unknown to her, a student waits politely nearby.

Jenna is about to make the discovery of her life. Not only does Dr. Carter acknowledge Jenna's presence, she does so with a bright, supportive and welcoming manner. Jenna feels relieved that she waited to speak with her instructor.

"Great, Jenna! I have been looking forward to speaking with you. You are a new student here, are you not?" Jenna nods quietly. Dr. Carter continues, "Well, I must say that **most students have the impression that the only time to see an instructor is when they have an illness or death in the family to report, or when their grades are so far gone that they are in a melt-down.**"

"Dr. Carter, I realize that I am new to college. And I am very much concerned that I do well in this class. It may be part of being new to the world of academe, but I am in a bit of a panic about the research assignment that I must do. I am hoping that you might have some suggestions that could help me refine my research topic. Can you help?"

"Believe it or not, I felt panicky when I started college here years ago. I did what you are doing. **It is a real honor to help you!**"

"WHEN SOMEONE SHOWS YOU WHO THEY ARE, BELIEVE THEM THE FIRST TIME." —OPRAH WINFREY

Grade Grabber Exercise

(QUICKLY SCAN THIS EXERCISE. JOT DOWN IDEAS, IF YOU WISH. READ THE NEXT PAGE. WRITE OR ADD TO YOUR RESPONSES BELOW. GAIN INSIGHT—TAKE ACTION!)

1. Do you normally find it easy or difficult to receive feedback from others? Explain.

2. How might outstanding and mediocre students view mistakes differently? Give examples.

3. In what way can mistakes trigger as well as deepen your sense of discovery and learning?

4. Can feedback based on what your instructor wants, in addition to what the course demands, be of value to you? Explain.

Pay Attention to Instructor Feedback

Professional opinions can give you the clues you need to succeed.

Would you be pleased if the suggestions that your instructor offered you contributed to your earning a significantly better grade? Of course you would. Not only that, but you would likely value your instructor all the more and also look forward to future feedback, even if you had to make an office appointment to get it.

Top students commonly exhibit these same behaviors. They realize that learning from mistakes is an important key to success. Paying attention to instructor feedback gives clues to a success path that many mediocre students refuse to consider or follow.

Notice the important dynamics at work here:

1. Instructors intend comments to demonstrate how they
    a. Assess the structure and logic of your paper.
    b. Weigh the merits of your paper's content.
    c. Want you to approach future course work.
    d. Award an overall grade.
2. Outstanding students use instructor comments to
    a. See what works and should be developed.
    b. See what does not work and should be cut.
    c. Eliminate otherwise unforeseen problems.
    d. Increase the chance of earning a top grade.
3. Mediocre students perceive instructor comments as
    a. A personal attack.
    b. Useless.
    c. Biased.
    d. A way of compromising the grade they deserve.

Dismissing what most top students see as critical information, mediocre students routinely ignore instructor comments. Why?

"A MAN WHO HAS COMMITTED A MISTAKE AND DOES NOT CORRECT IT IS COMMITTING ANOTHER MISTAKE." —CONFUCIUS

Grade Grabber Exercise

(QUICKLY SCAN THIS EXERCISE. JOT DOWN ADDITIONAL IDEAS, IF YOU WISH. READ THE NEXT PAGE. RETURN TO THE FOLLOWING SUGGESTIONS. GAIN INSIGHT—TAKE ACTION!)

1. Using the criteria from "Assume Assignments Have a Point," state why you think Student A earned a top grade, while Student B received a zero on this project. Give two examples.

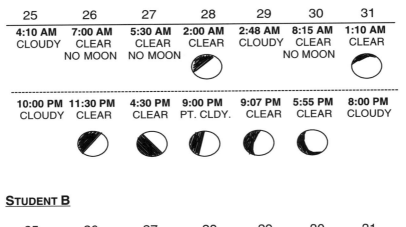

STUDENT A

25	26	27	28	29	30	31
4:10 AM	7:00 AM	5:30 AM	2:00 AM	2:48 AM	8:15 AM	1:10 AM
CLOUDY	CLEAR	CLEAR	CLEAR	CLOUDY	CLEAR	CLEAR
	NO MOON	NO MOON			NO MOON	

10:00 PM	11:30 PM	4:30 PM	9:00 PM	9:07 PM	5:55 PM	8:00 PM
CLOUDY	CLEAR	CLEAR	PT. CLDY.	CLEAR	CLEAR	CLOUDY

STUDENT B

25	26	27	28	29	30	31
8:10 AM	8:07 AM	8:31 AM	8:20 AM	8:40 AM	8:11 AM	8:17 AM
CLOUDY	CLEAR	CLEAR	CLEAR	CLOUDY	CLEAR	CLEAR

10:10 PM	10:50 PM	10:23 PM	9:50 PM	9:47 PM	9:55 PM	9:40 PM
CLOUDY	CLEAR	CLEAR	CLOUDY	CLEAR	CLEAR	CLOUDY

Assume All Assignments Have a Point

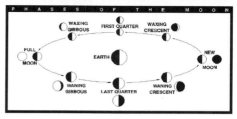

Evading serious effort seriously destroys learning.

You undoubtedly know the saying, "Little things mean a lot." While most **top students are open to smarter ways of doing things,** these same students are **also very wary of taking the easy way** out. Have you ever been tempted to cut corners — even a little? **When cutting corners replaces serious effort, disaster is never very far off.**

Fatima, an outstanding student, attends the first of Dr. Adams' two astronomy classes. Bill, a mediocre student, attends the second. Dr. Adams requires his students to record the moon's phases twice daily. Fatima decides to give it her best effort. Bill rejects the idea as a waste of time.

Several months go by. As the end of the semester draws near, a friend introduces Bill to Fatima. During their conversation, he discovers that they are both taking Dr. Adams' astronomy class. When Fatima tells him that she has been **carefully following Dr. Adams' instructions,** Bill cannot believe his ears.

"What's the point?" he moans. "Why should I bother making sketches of phases of the moon twice a day when I can copy them from the chart on the classroom wall?"

Fatima responds, "That's what I thought at first. But then I realized that **no university awards degrees for mindless busywork.** Didn't you read the instructions?" With that, she shows Bill a notebook containing her astronomy observations.

As he reviews her work, Bill is overcome by a sense of guilt and dread. Not only did Fatima include dates, times, weather and visibility conditions, but she also indicated whether or not the moon was visible. Bill's notes clearly lacked these details. He realizes that when he decided not to follow instructions, he had cut one too many corners. "What do I do now?"

"HOW TEDIOUS IS A GUILTY CONSCIENCE!" —JOHN WEBSTER

Grade Grabber Exercise

(QUICKLY SCAN THIS EXERCISE. JOT DOWN IDEAS, IF YOU WISH. READ THE NEXT PAGE. WRITE OR ADD TO YOUR RESPONSES BELOW. GAIN INSIGHT—TAKE ACTION!)

1. Judy tells you that she is going to ask questions right away, rather than wait until the lecture ends. What, if anything, would you tell her?

2. What types of student questions most impress instructors?

3. From your own observation, why do mediocre students do poorly during in-class question-and-answer sessions?

Know When to Ask Questions

By giving lecturers what they need, you can more safely pin down the answer to virtually any question.

Do you want to earn the most points possible for your in-class effort? Would you like to know how the best students ask the right question at the right time to consistently impress their instructors? Does your instructor's offer of end-of-semester bonus points sound attractive to you? If so, read on.

Be sure to find out your instructor's policy, procedures and expectations regarding students' in-class questions — and do it on the first day of class. Never naïvely assume that all instructors share the same outlook regarding student questions. They do not.

You can make a positive, strong and lasting impact on your instructor's opinion of your work and of your value to the class by considering the following suggestions:

1. Stick to the time(s) and guidelines your instructor reserves for student questions. An instructor may allot:
   a. A time slot immediately following the lecture.
   b. Unrestricted use of questions and answers during the entire lecture.
2. Accurately record and intelligently refer to your notes.
3. Ask questions that seek to sharpen your understanding.
4. Formulate questions that intelligently tie lecture content to other course work and reading.

Be aware that your instructor seeks questions that demonstrate both your study and in-class value. Carefully preread prior to each class as top students do. Poor students do not bother. Inevitably, ill-informed student questions force instructors to pin them down: "You did not bother reading for this class, did you?"

"IGNORANT MEN RAISE QUESTIONS THAT WISE MEN ANSWERED A THOUSAND YEARS AGO." —JOHANN WOLFGANG VON GOETHE

Grade Grabber Exercise

(QUICKLY SCAN THIS EXERCISE. JOT DOWN IDEAS, IF
YOU WISH. READ THE NEXT PAGE. WRITE OR ADD TO
YOUR RESPONSES BELOW. GAIN INSIGHT—TAKE ACTION!)

1. Write down four or five one-word reasons for avoiding the use of slang in verbal or written classwork.

2. What is the role of slang in daily life? Do intelligent people ever use slang? Explain.

3. Name two things you can do to increase your chances for a top grade during in-class discussions or written assignments.

4. Imagine an instructor with a reputation for being "way cool." Can you assume that non-collegiate terms are acceptable in his class? Explain.

Express Yourself Intelligently

A verbal or written response is not the time for "Yada, yada, yada."

Do you want to get top grades? Do you think that intelligently expressed verbal or written responses are necessary to get them? Of course! Incredibly, many mediocre students resort to using slang, inappropriate or otherwise bankrupt expressions within an academic setting. Even more troubling, these same students are frequently clueless as to the impact of their words on their grades.

By contrast, almost all outstanding students strive to intelligently express themselves. They think through their words before responding. They strictly avoid all verbal or written slang. You can, too, if you approach your work with the right attitude.

If sounding "way cool" is more important to you than sounding collegiate, then you might just as well say, "Hasta la vista, baby!" to a good grade. By limiting your responses to well-articulated, college-level English, your instructor is much more likely to notice and to reward your:

1. Thoughtfulness.
2. Precision.
3. Use of course terminology.
4. Completeness.

Slang is everywhere. Sports broadcasts flood the airwaves with buzz words, makeshift expressions and clichés. Words and expressions from sitcoms, pop music, informal conversations with family and friends, etc., can be fatal when used in an academic setting. No matter how "cool" your instructor may be, do not assume that substandard work is acceptable. It never is.

Words have power. Make certain that the words you use in a classroom setting contain the power to intelligently promote your best interests. Words can send your instructor the wrong message.

"THE MEDIUM IS THE MESSAGE." —MARSHALL MCLUHAN

Grade Grabber Exercise

(QUICKLY SCAN THIS EXERCISE. JOT DOWN IDEAS, IF
YOU WISH. READ THE NEXT PAGE. WRITE OR ADD TO
YOUR RESPONSES BELOW. GAIN INSIGHT—TAKE ACTION!)

1. Have you ever received a particularly rude e-mail from someone? How did it make you feel? Explain.

2. Why is it best to delay sending an e-mail that is written in anger? Is there ever a time when it is wise not to delay?

3. Most instructors value e-mail that is clear, specific and respectful of their time. What is your approach?

4. What steps can you take to ensure that your e-mails are received and handled by your instructor in a timely manner?

Watch Your E-Mail Etiquette

Never send your instructor e-mail that will backfire on you.

Would you consider it a violation of professional etiquette if your instructor sent you an e-mail that was crudely written, blunt, angry, vague or insulting to you? What sorts of negative labels would pop into your head if a fellow student sent you an odd and demanding e-mail? You can join the ranks of outstanding students who protect their reputations for professionalism and courtesy. Does a good reputation sound worth protecting?

We all make judgments based on etiquette, be it in the quest for a job, a friendship, a sweetheart or any other worthwhile goal. In all of these cases, and many more, the minimum gestures of common courtesy always make a difference. Is it any wonder that the French word for "label" is "etiquette"? What is your label?

Whether we are seeking to promote ourselves in work, social or academic circles, a certain measure of professional courtesy should always be in place. Those are the rules of civilized living.

Incredibly, many students who might otherwise positively impress their instructors sabotage themselves with their own e-mail messages. You can avoid joining their ranks if you:

1. Taste your own words. Never send an e-mail in anger.
2. Choose your words carefully and intelligently.
    a. "Dear Ms. Smith" or "Dear Mr. Jones" or "In conclusion," or "I look forward to your response" impress instructors.
    b. "hi," "Hi," "Hey, dude," or "N.E.way," or "Get back, okay? Gotta run." annoy instructors.
3. Write e-mail that is both clear and to the point.
4. Have a sharp friend proof all of your e-mail for errors.
5. Allow your instructor adequate time to respond.
6. Be honest. Be open. Be reliable. When in doubt, follow up.

"COURTESY ON ONE SIDE CAN NEVER LAST LONG." —PROVERB

Grade Grabber Exercise

(QUICKLY SCAN THIS EXERCISE. JOT DOWN IDEAS, IF YOU WISH. READ THE NEXT PAGE. WRITE OR ADD TO YOUR RESPONSES BELOW. GAIN INSIGHT—TAKE ACTION!)

1. What is a mentor? Can anyone fill this role? Explain.

2. What are some ways that mentors might work with and/or interact with you? What sorts of assistance should they offer?

3. How long does it take to develop the mentor-student relationship? Is it a one-way relationship? Discuss.

4. List some important differences between good and poor mentoring.

Benefit from a Mentor

Many professionals are willing to coach
serious students with insights and support.

Would you like to propel yourself light-years
ahead of your normal learning curve? You can by
developing a relationship with a mentor, as many top students do.
Whether or not you plan on earning an advanced degree, the right
mentor can have a positive impact on your future.

Why is mentoring superior to attending classes and leaving it
at that? Mentoring puts a thoroughly seasoned expert into a
professional (even collegial) relationship with a student. Through
discussion, feedback and the mentor's personal example, the finer
points of a specific academic discipline are more effectively and
lastingly impressed on the student.

While no professional is required to become involved in
mentoring, a student should be able to recognize those traits that
best serve his or her ongoing needs. As a professional two-way
relationship, mentoring takes time, even years, to develop fully.

While it is the rare person whose mentoring style does not
need a bit of "fine tuning" from time to time, review and evaluate
the following table for mentoring traits that are critical to your
needs. A good mentor will consistently offer a hand of support.

GOOD MENTORING	POOR MENTORING
1. In-depth experience	1. Insufficient experience
2. Values you as mentee	2. Values being a mentor
3. Supports progress	3. Supports own interest
4. Strongest over time	4. Strongest at the start
5. Committed to your long-term growth	5. Lacks commitment to your long-term growth
6. Mature reliability	6. Unreliable or evasive

"YOU CANNOT SHAKE HANDS WITH A CLENCHED FIST."
—INDIRA GANDHI

Part 4

Turn Information into Learning

Grade Grabber Exercise

(QUICKLY SCAN THIS EXERCISE. JOT DOWN IDEAS, IF YOU WISH. READ THE NEXT PAGE. WRITE OR ADD TO YOUR RESPONSES BELOW. GAIN INSIGHT—TAKE ACTION!)

1. Doodle this Egyptian "cartouche" drawing in the space provided on the right. Sloppy is good. What counts is memorable, useful notation.

2. Doodle "Whistler's Mother." Nothing fancy. Suggest the footstool, the chair's leg, the picture on the wall and the contrast between the hands, head and bonnet against her dark clothing.

Trigger Your Recall

Increase your odds and make the grade with simple doodling.

You should be aware of the fact that the most basic art appreciation course you may take presents a different set of note-taking challenges. These challenges may be vastly different from any others you may experience as a student. But you can be ready for them, starting right now.

Ask yourself: Do you want to get the best grade possible? If so, you need to adopt a more sophisticated approach when verbal and visual note-taking tasks are merged. If you are not particularly "artistic," here is good news.

Doodling should be part of your note-taking arsenal because:

- Doodling is fun.
- Doodling is a powerful learning tool for study and recall.
- Everybody can doodle!

To illustrate this point, let's pretend that as part of your instructor's slide lecture on Leonardo DaVinci's "Mona Lisa," you learn that DaVinci was famous for using the "Golden Triangle" layout in his paintings. Simply make an intelligent "doodle" of the Mona Lisa, and highlight/note the "Golden Triangle" as part of your regular notation.

That's it!

This method will heighten the use of both sides of your brain (left logical/right visual) while greatly increasing your ability to trigger recall during later study, review and test taking. (Share this tip with a study pal!) Do it!

Leonardo and Mona would surely praise your efforts with that greatest of all Italian endorsements: "Atsa nice!"

"SIMPLICITY IS THE ULTIMATE SOPHISTICATION."
—LEONARDO DAVINCI

Grade Grabber Exercise

(QUICKLY SCAN THIS EXERCISE. JOT DOWN IDEAS, IF
YOU WISH. READ THE NEXT PAGE. WRITE OR ADD TO
YOUR RESPONSES BELOW. GAIN INSIGHT—TAKE ACTION!)

1. Picture yourself as a news interviewer. List five or six skills
   you would need to record outstanding, focused and valuable
   notes.

2. Recall important news bulletins that you have seen or heard.
   How did they manage to grab your attention? What sorts of
   reactions did they create in you? Explain.

3. What six words can help you ask better questions and follow-
   up questions when you take in-class lecture notes?

4. How do "active" interviewing and note-taking skills apply to
   active reading? Jot down some suggestions. Start applying your
   best insights to increase your ability to master course material.

Visualize Lectures as TV Interviews

Television journalists show you how you can take "live" notes.

"We interrupt this program for a **Breaking News Bulletin.**" What happens when you hear these words? It is the same thing that happens to nearly anyone who hears them, right? Bells go off. **Who? What? When? Where? Why? How? questions** immediately dominate your thinking, create a sense of urgency and naturally focus and **stimulate** your ongoing interest in organizing the information for later recall. Consider the following suggestions that, seen within the framework of a news report, can help you improve your attitude and take better lecture notes as well.

Attention: Picture a "Breaking News Bulletin" that only shows a newscaster sitting at his desk giving a report about a huge apartment fire that raises more questions than it answers. Next, imagine yourself changing channels. **Urgency:** The next network has a "live" camera crew covering the story, interviewing a burn victim who provides answers to key story questions. **Interest:** As the story unfolds, you learn more information about the fire. More people are inside, an elderly invalid is trapped on the top floor and a helicopter is heard just outside of camera range.

"5 Ws-and-the-H Questions": You can create an astonishing number of useful questions with six simple words. **Who** is being affected? **What** more can be done? **When** will more assistance arrive? **Where** will it be coming from? **Why** did the smoke detectors not work? **How** much time do they need to get the remaining people out of the building?

You may never conduct a television interview. But recalling the image of breaking television news coverage can add spark and inspiration to your in-class note taking and follow-up questions. You can seize control of your destiny and take charge of your notes, even if the lecture is not as exciting as a five-alarm fire.

"NOTHING IS MORE TERRIBLE THAN ACTIVITY WITHOUT INSIGHT."
—THOMAS CARLYLE

Grade Grabber Exercise

(QUICKLY SCAN THIS EXERCISE. JOT DOWN IDEAS, IF YOU WISH. READ THE NEXT PAGE. WRITE OR ADD TO YOUR RESPONSES BELOW. GAIN INSIGHT—TAKE ACTION!)

1. Imagine that you have just taken your best lecture notes ever. Name two specific things you have learned to do differently.

2. Do top students tend to take a lot of notes or few notes? Explain.

3. What is a quick way to spot mediocre notes?

4. How might you more quickly improve your note-taking ability?

Take Complete Lecture Notes

Most instructors agree that poor note-taking skills can sabotage your semester.

Imagine the following scenario. You find yourself sitting in a lecture class, feverishly working away at your notes. You clearly want to do well in this course. Every student near you senses it!

You wonder, "How much time do I have?" Bearing down on yourself, you look up from your work. Only a minute—maybe two—remains. Your instructor makes his last comments; and just as he gestures to make his final point, you realize that your hard work is paying off. These are **your best lecture notes ever.** Of course, there have been clues all along. Neighboring students have expressed an interest in getting together for a study session to "go over notes." They realize that nothing of value comes easily.

Education is work. If you want to increase your grade point average, you can. **Get into the habit of taking more, not fewer, notes—then use them. To do otherwise is to risk self-sabotage.**

Effective note takers consistently retain more information, cultivate a better understanding of the material and regularly outdistance those who have poor note-taking habits. When you have more material to work with, it becomes a relatively simple matter to sort, organize and condense the key information that you will need for course mastery. Inadequate lecture notes provide no such option.

Keep in mind that unless a specific quotation, rule, principle, formula, etc. needs to be noted verbatim, you can learn to effectively capture the core elements of most lecture content. **Practice, careful attention and "comparing notes" with top students can help your note-taking skills to soar.** You can do well if you put your mind and effort into improved note taking.

Poor students are often inattentive and take too few notes. They invite failure. Would you invite them to improve your grades?

"I THINK THE ONE LESSON I HAVE LEARNED IS THAT THERE IS NO SUBSTITUTE FOR PAYING ATTENTION." —DIANE SAWYER

Grade Grabber Exercise

(QUICKLY SCAN THIS EXERCISE. JOT DOWN IDEAS, IF YOU WISH. READ THE NEXT PAGE. WRITE OR ADD TO YOUR RESPONSES BELOW. GAIN INSIGHT—TAKE ACTION!)

1. Honestly rate yourself on a scale from one to five. How committed are you to doing whatever work needs to be done to be a successful student?

   Barely   1   2   3   4   5   Totally

2. What is the purpose of prereading a text? How does prereading improve your ability to master information? Give examples.

3. In what way does attending all classes maximize your ability to create stronger connections and get more from your reading?

4. Write down five to ten ideas that can help you to better predict and prepare for test content. Isolate the one idea that could help you most. How specifically can this help you to perform better?

Track Important, Testable Information

Alert prereading, note taking and logic can enable you to more confidently predict test content.

Do you want to increase your effectiveness, take charge of your studies and direct your path to ever greater success? You can. All you need is a little preparation, attentiveness to detail and a willingness to draw intelligent conclusions for yourself.

The following steps can help you to more confidently predict, organize and master the content of an upcoming test:

1. **Get with the program. Refer to your syllabus regularly.**
    a. Make a habit of regularly referring to the semester guidelines and schedule found in your syllabus to keep you on track and out of hot water.
2. **Preread and master assigned class readings.**
    a. Note key points, terms, concepts, formulas, etc.
    b. Prepare any important questions you wish to ask your instructor during class.
3. **Attend all class lectures. Be sure to note**
    a. Material that matches key reading points.
    b. Original lecture content that ties in to your reading.
    c. Key lecture material not found in your reading.
    d. Handouts, videos, etc. that complement b. and c.
    e. Strong and/or repeated lecture points or obvious statements, such as, "That is the sort of thing that you might find on a test."
4. **Routinely review your notes immediately after class** by yourself and/or with a study partner.
5. **Ask your instructor for possible test study suggestions.** Such suggestions cannot cover everything you will need to know, so trust your instincts. Always go the extra mile.
6. **Prepare well.** It is a major source of academic power.

"AN IMPORTANT KEY TO SELF-CONFIDENCE IS PREPARATION."
—ARTHUR ASHE

Grade Grabber Exercise

(QUICKLY SCAN THIS EXERCISE. JOT DOWN IDEAS, IF YOU WISH. READ THE NEXT PAGE. WRITE OR ADD TO YOUR RESPONSES BELOW. GAIN INSIGHT—TAKE ACTION!)

1. What is critical thinking?

2. Your favorite late-night comedian performs a monologue in which a statesman is mercilessly criticized. Is this an example of critical thinking? Explain.

3. Why do you conclude that critical thinking is required in so many areas of academic study? Give two examples.

4. Based on what you know about critical thinking, indicate six professions in which such thinking is especially important. (Example: Medicine.)

Develop Your Own Critical Thinking Skills

Your willingness to think things through is more important than a high I.Q.

Many first-year students confuse cynical thinking with critical thinking. Top students are conscious of the difference and capitalize on this knowledge to achieve higher grades.

Cynical thinking takes a scornful, pessimistic and unresourceful approach towards most, if not all, information presented. **Critical thinking** involves a conscious, deliberate and measured suspension of personal judgment and/or opinion in order to maximize the value of academic enquiry.

Consider why critical thinking is demanded by instructors:

CRITICAL THINKING PROMOTES	CYNICAL THINKING PROMOTES
1. Objectivity	1. Subjectivity
2. Flexibility	2. Rigidity
3. Closer questioning	3. Closed questioning
4. Understanding	4. Definitions
5. Better information	5. Limited information
6. Fairness	6. Dismissiveness
7. Evaluative sense	7. Manipulation of data
8. Unexpected findings	8. Predictable answers
9. Integrated judgment	9. Biased judgment
10. Better research ideas	10. Research bankruptcy

Note that critical thinking is your key to writing or "arguing" quality academic papers (Steps 1-9). Skillful closing remarks, tied to possible future research (Step 10), can critically promote you!

"WHO QUESTIONS MUCH SHALL LEARN MUCH AND RETAIN MUCH."
—SIR FRANCIS BACON

Grade Grabber Exercise

(QUICKLY SCAN THIS EXERCISE. JOT DOWN IDEAS, IF
YOU WISH. READ THE NEXT PAGE. WRITE OR ADD TO
YOUR RESPONSES BELOW. GAIN INSIGHT—TAKE ACTION!)

1. How does being familiar with the Socratic Method give you an advantage in the classroom?

2. What might confuse unsuspecting students about the Socratic interview?

3. How might a Socratic interview be used? What is the Socratic interview supposed to reveal?

4. What is the best way to prepare for a Socratic interview?

Prepare for the Socratic Method

It is time to think more carefully whenever your professors become professedly "ignorant."

The ancient Greek teacher-philosopher, Socrates, developed a deceptively simple question-and-answer teaching approach that is so powerful it continues to be used in college and university classrooms. Known as the Socratic Method, or Socratic Interview, a hallmark of this learning approach rests in its reversal of roles.

In the Socratic Method it is you, not your instructor, who must be fully prepared, engaged and ready to convey knowledge. It is your instructor's role to ask questions that reveal the depth of your learning mastery. Such an interview can take place during a class discussion or as part of a formally scheduled presentation.

Consider the following example of how your instructor might use the Socratic Method as a means of separating error from truth:

1. Student is fully prepared to present knowledge mastery.
2. Instructor professes ignorance of such knowledge.
3. Instructor seeks instruction through a series of questions.
4. Student often admits and recants defective knowledge.
5. Student often admits and refines deficient knowledge.
6. Instructor continues until sufficient insight is revealed.

The Socratic Method immediately exposes student learning or the lack of it. Keep in mind that, although your instructor may be "professing ignorance," the quest for instruction is real. Be prepared. Respond in a simple, straightforward and thoughtful manner.

You cannot make the grade by "winging it." Hesitancy accompanied by an inexcusable lack of knowledge can become a transparent Socratic liability — more poisonous than hemlock.

"OH, I GET IT. YOU WANT TO KNOW WHAT I THINK!"
—ANONYMOUS FIRST-YEAR STUDENT

Grade Grabber Exercise

(QUICKLY SCAN THIS EXERCISE. JOT DOWN IDEAS, IF
YOU WISH. READ THE NEXT PAGE. WRITE OR ADD TO
YOUR RESPONSES BELOW. GAIN INSIGHT—TAKE ACTION!)

1. What triggers boredom in you?

2. How do you stay alert when you become bored?

3. Bored students usually earn mediocre grades. What traits
   could cause your instructor to grade students downward?

4. What could you do to be a standout student and maximize
   your grade for in-class participation?

Banish Boredom Before You Get Bored "Dumb"!

Bored students are usually boring— and clueless. You don't have to be.

Do you ever get bored? Everybody does—even "A" students. But when it comes to actually doing something about it, successful and poor students part company.

Would you like to stop boredom in its tracks? If so, here are some smart tips to follow.

First, acknowledge boredom as soon as it hits. Then you can do something about it. Consider what actions you can take to defeat it. Do not fall prey to complaining.

Second, picture yourself as proactive, energetic and resourceful. Your mind and demeanor will begin to rally around it. Avoid clueless passivity that leads to being bored "dumb."

PROACTIVE	BORED "DUMB"
1. Stimulating	1. Uninspiring
2. Fully prepared	2. Unprepared
3. Perceptive	3. Clueless
4. Committed	4. Neutral
5. Enquiring	5. Inert
6. Involved	6. Detached
7. Alert	7. Sleepy
8. Focused	8. Generalizing

Third, top students use positive inner statements, such as "Break's over!" or "It's up to me!" to energize themselves and defeat self-pity and boredom. Poor students whine, "Give me a break!" Which kind of student do you want to be?

"IF I HAVE EVER MADE ANY VALUABLE DISCOVERIES, IT HAS BEEN OWING MORE TO PATIENT ATTENTION THAN TO ANY OTHER TALENT."
—ISAAC NEWTON

Grade Grabber Exercise

(QUICKLY SCAN THIS EXERCISE. JOT DOWN ADDITIONAL IDEAS, IF YOU WISH. READ THE NEXT PAGE. RETURN TO THE FOLLOWING SUGGESTIONS. GAIN INSIGHT—TAKE ACTION!)

1. How often do you choose to sit at the front of the classroom?

    Never   1   2   3   4   5   Always

2. Why do you think most people tend to stay in the same seats all semester? Are there advantages and disadvantages to this approach? Give four or five examples.

3. Imagine you are seated in the front row and a friend calls you from the back of the room to join him. Assuming that you are seated forward to make learning easier on yourself, what is the likelihood that you will move and join your friend?

    None   1   2   3   4   5   Guaranteed

4. What goes through your mind when you choose a seat on the first day of the class? How might auditoriums, labs, etc. present unique seating challenges and/or benefits? Explain.

Sit in the Front Row
Becoming a top student means
never taking a back seat to success.

Study after study reveals that, on average, those who sit in the front row of the classroom tend to earn higher grades than those seated behind them. Why?

A side-by-side look should provide some insight:

FRONT ROW SEATING TENDS TO PROMOTE	DISTANCED SEATING TENDS TO FOSTER
1. Preparedness	1. Less or no preparation
2. Mature accountability	2. Group conformity
3. Active participation	3. Disconnectedness
4. Concentration	4. Distraction
5. Prompt instructor help	5. Delayed instructor help
6. Improved rapport	6. Awkward interaction
7. Clear sightlines	7. Obstructed sightlines
8. Auditory clarity	8. Difficulty hearing
9. Self-confidence	9. Uneasiness when called
10. Memorability	10. Anonymity
11. A positive impression	11. A mixed impression
12. Attendance	12. Absence

Of course, it is always possible to earn top grades without sitting in the front row. Notice, however, that the same traits you need to succeed are easier to cultivate and maintain when you move forward. That is why so many outstanding students can be seen sitting in the first row of most classrooms. They want to focus on performing at a consistently high level, and they will not take a back seat to success. Why not go to the head of the class?

"CONCENTRATE ALL YOUR THOUGHTS UPON THE WORK AT HAND. THE SUN'S RAYS DO NOT BURN UNTIL BROUGHT TO A FOCUS."
—ALEXANDER GRAHAM BELL

Part 5

Jumpstart Your Personal Study Time

Grade Grabber Exercise

(QUICKLY SCAN THIS EXERCISE. JOT DOWN IDEAS, IF YOU WISH. READ THE NEXT PAGE. WRITE OR ADD TO YOUR RESPONSES BELOW. GAIN INSIGHT—TAKE ACTION!)

1. A visually appealing room can support study, while an unpleasant one can undercut it. What is your experience?

2. Recall your favorite study area. What does your choice tell you about your level of commitment to college work? Explain.

3. Picture your least productive study area. What simple things might you do to use it more effectively?

4. List several ways to eliminate interruptions during study time. Take action today on one of them.

Use High-Octane Study Zones

Instantly deepen your mastery by choosing the best places to study.

Your place of study can have an enormous impact on your grades. Why do so many students perform below their true abilities? Often they simply ignore the importance of seeking out the most brain-friendly environments. Where do you study?

The great American architect, Louis Henri Sullivan, understood the importance of matching the right environment to the right task. This insight evolved into a principle. That principle became the foundation and driving force for all of his work— "Form follows function."

The best students occasionally rethink their study habits. They also ask questions about which study areas should be kept, modified or totally eliminated. The reasoning is simple: "Form follows function." While work, home and other areas may not be ideal, you need to establish optimum "study zones" for yourself— places where you do your best studying. Consider the following:

- Study at another campus. Unfamiliarity with students can contribute to increased concentration and subject mastery.
- Start a study group and meet regularly at the library.
- Claim your own exclusive academic zone(s) in your home or office. After a while, the power of the specific associated habit will grow and reinforce your positive feelings and sense of progress. You may choose to "encode" your study places, breaking them down by task:
  - Dining room table used only for note taking.
  - Desk used only for word processing.
  - Company conference room used only for reading.
  - Kitchen table used only for preparing for tests.
- Add to and reshape your own list of study locations.

"WE SHAPE OUR BUILDINGS AND THEY SHAPE US."
—WINSTON CHURCHILL

Grade Grabber Exercise

(QUICKLY SCAN THIS EXERCISE. JOT DOWN IDEAS, IF
YOU WISH. READ THE NEXT PAGE. WRITE OR ADD TO
YOUR RESPONSES BELOW. GAIN INSIGHT—TAKE ACTION!)

1. What is your favorite way to take notes as you read?

2. Is your ability to read and retrieve information helped
   or hindered by marking your textbook? How?

3. Do you think that personal study materials should always
   be kept as neat as possible for resale? Support your response.

4. In what ways do you review and/or modify your approach
   to reading and learning? Has it changed over time? Explain.

Retrieve Information Like an Airedale

Your textbook can be a winner, even when it looks like a "dog's dinner."

No bones about it, you would never submit a paper that resembles the proverbial "dog's dinner" and expect a great grade. High standards for content and neatness are strictly required. Yet whatever you decide to do with your personal study materials is pretty much up to you. And why not?

When you choose to mark up your textbook, who cares how neat looking it is, except a used book salesman? Your instructor almost certainly does not. The point is to do what works best for you. Realize the enormous role top grades have on your lifelong earnings. Never lower your grade-earning ability in the quest for "chump change." Decide from an intellectual perspective and then from a retail point of view. Respect your strengths and limitations.

Consider two types of students who elect not to write in their books. The first group leaves them untouched primarily because such students retain information better by writing in notebooks, etc. In contrast, the second group's one focus is a better book buy-back price. Fatally lacking the skills of the previous group, the second group of students will jeopardize its grades — even when writing and highlighting in their textbooks could bring success.

No matter how "dogged" your preferred learning style is, make certain that your note-taking approach to reading and study

- Reinforces efficiency and in-depth learning.
- Eases, encourages and empowers your later review.
- Helps you to locate information in a flash.
- Pinpoints interconnections between texts, lectures and your other course materials.
- Can assist your retrieval of key formulas and other details.

"IF YOU THINK DOGS CAN'T COUNT, TRY PUTTING THREE DOG BISCUITS IN YOUR POCKET AND THEN GIVING FIDO ONLY TWO OF THEM."
—PHIL PASTORET

Grade Grabber Exercise

(QUICKLY SCAN THIS EXERCISE. JOT DOWN IDEAS, IF YOU WISH. READ THE NEXT PAGE. WRITE OR ADD TO YOUR RESPONSES BELOW. GAIN INSIGHT—TAKE ACTION!)

1. Price aside, what do you usually look for when you buy a used book?

2. What would cause you not to buy a particular used book?

3. Professor Jane Scott loans a prized, out-of-print book to Robert, who is a student in one of her classes. Within days, Robert loses the book and dutifully reports the loss. Although clearly annoyed at his carelessness, she assures him that she attached no sentimental value to the book. Nevertheless, Robert is surprised to learn that his offer to locate and buy a replacement copy in "mint" condition will never fully replace the one that he lost. Explain.

Power Up Your Reading Time

The right used book can light up your way and speed up your learning.

Would you like to pull victory out of a pile of used books? You can. Although many students buy used books on a regular basis, top students often look for smart ways to exploit such purchases.

At one time or another, most students are forced to purchase a used book for class. Very often this is because the title is out of print. Students might also be forced to buy used books when new book inventories are hopelessly sold out. Of course, some students buy used books primarily to "save money." Regardless of the need, many outstanding students carefully examine scribbled and/or highlighted books whenever they buy used books.

Why would high academic performers select books that are marked up? Momentum speeds mastery. While sloppy, hard-to-read used books are liabilities to be avoided, intelligently marked books can offer more insights than newly published ones.

Think about it. Perceptively marked books contain bonuses in notation, highlighting, underlining, etc. As a trailblazer of sorts, the original reader's reactions can inspire you to learn more, faster. They can stimulate your appreciation for or disagreement with the previous owner's thinking processes and observations. Key lecture points are occasionally buried in the marginal notes of used books. By considering any markings as potential clues, rather than answers written in stone, you should do just fine.

Good used books can activate:

- The sense of having a study partner reading with you.
- New ways to do your own marking, underlining, etc.
- New ways to take and organize notes while you read.
- Your own ideas, insights and understanding.

"THE BEST EFFECT OF ANY BOOK IS THAT IT EXCITES THE READER TO SELF-ACTIVITY." —THOMAS CARLYLE

Grade Grabber Exercise

(QUICKLY SCAN THIS EXERCISE. JOT DOWN ADDITIONAL
IDEAS, IF YOU WISH. READ THE NEXT PAGE. RETURN TO
THE FOLLOWING SUGGESTIONS. GAIN INSIGHT—TAKE ACTION!)

1. Select keywords and search for images based on your assigned reading. Use a top search engine (i.e. Google™, YAHOO!®). **Look for keywords in the Table of Contents, Subject Index and Introduction** of your assigned text. Check your **lecture notes and handouts**, as well.

2. **PC** web browser and word processor **protocols** can vary. Use the "Help" menu tab or ask a computer lab expert to assist you.

   Copy a web image, if authorized. Move your mouse's cursor (it may appear in the shape of a hand or an arrow) to the middle of the image you wish to copy. Click your mouse's **right button**. A drop-down options menu will appear. Select "Copy."
   Paste your image inside your Microsoft Word® or similar **word processing document notes**. Open your word processing document. Place your word processor's insertion point ("I beam") where you wish to paste your image. Select Edit and Paste. The image automatically loads inside your document.
   Next, place your mouse's cursor in the middle of the image. Click the right button. A drop-down menu appears. Choose "**Format Picture**...." A tabbed group of options appears. Select the "Layout" tab. Select "Square" under a category called "Wrapping Style." Push the OK button. The tabbed group options disappear, bringing you back to the image inside your document.
   Place your mouse's cursor over the middle of the image and left click your mouse. "**Resizing** Handles" appear along the outer image edges. Place the cursor over a corner handle until the single arrow takes on a double arrow appearance. Depress and hold your left mouse button. A dragging motion allows you to resize the image, while it remains stationary.
   Repositioning the image inside your document is easy. Place your mouse's cursor over the middle of the image. Depress and hold the left mouse button as you drag and move your image to any new spot within your study document.

Illustrate Any Text with Web Search Images

Internet graphics can boost learning and mastery.

Text happens. Reading conditions are not always user friendly. **Many top students know first hand how stress, fatigue, illness or other negative factors can rob your brain of processing power—the very thing you need to succeed.** This can undercut your reading skills and threaten your grades. Once that happens, even the most interesting reading assignments become painfully difficult, if not impossible, burdens.

Here is a hint that can easily get you back on track to reading power and proficiency. **Use keyword internet image searches to graphically illustrate your reading.** Such images can quickly get your mind back into focus. And they can be true lifesavers when all else fails.

Get on the internet. Access a first-rate search engine, such as Google™ or YAHOO!® Select the tab marked "images." Type your first text keyword inside the "search images" window and press "search." A group of thumbnail-sized images appears. Double click on any that look helpful, memorable and informative.

The best images can spark renewed interest and zest for your reading assignment. When multiple browsers are opened, each successful search adds to your image gallery. Simply double click your web browser icon to initiate new keyword searches.

Is it possible to copy and insert images in your word processing notes? It can be, but it may not always be legal. Some images are in the public domain, allowing unlimited access and use. Other images are available for educational purposes only. Some sites demand that you request permission. Some sites charge. Still others strictly forbid downloading. (Check with your college library staff or computer lab supervisor for help.)

Above all, take the initiative. The universe seems to align itself with those who take action. No matter how difficult your reading may seem, text-related image searches can help to restore your stamina while graphically reactivating your focus and learning.

"THE SOUL CANNOT THINK WITHOUT A PICTURE." —ARISTOTLE

Grade Grabber Exercise

(QUICKLY SCAN THIS EXERCISE. JOT DOWN IDEAS, IF YOU WISH. READ THE NEXT PAGE. WRITE OR ADD TO YOUR RESPONSES BELOW. GAIN INSIGHT—TAKE ACTION!)

1. Mass-marketed sound is everywhere. What makes some "average-sounding" voices more powerful and memorable than others? (Examples: Tone, speed, emotion, accent, etc.)

2. How might audio recordings maximize your study output?

3. In what tasks might audio recordings not be your best option?

4. Several outstanding students have said that they could "hear" their audio recordings in their minds during exams. Do you think that repeated audio playbacks could do the same for you? Honestly rate yourself on a scale from one to five.

   Only geniuses can.   1   2   3   4   5   I can do this, too.

Become Your Own Audio-Learning Coach

Your voice triggers deep learning.

Most academic instructors will not allow you to make a sound recording of their lectures during class. The reason is simple. They want you to develop and/or sharpen your written note-taking skills, which will greatly increase your chances of mastering the material under study.

But what if you could include listening as part of your approach to learning? Happily, you can. Many experts agree that most of us prefer the sound of our own voice whenever we listen to deep-learning recordings.

Try it for yourself. Use the power of your voice to record your own compelling learning resources. Here are a few of the benefits:

1. Improved time management.
2. Better learning and recall.
3. Reduced stress.

You can reserve a block of time each week to convert your notes into sound recordings. Forget perfection. You are recording to learn. Read for yourself. Your recording time doubles as review time. You are deepening your knowledge of course material in a very powerful way.

You are in for incredible discoveries in learning and recall the moment you take yourself and your future seriously. First of all, the actual experience of creating your own material helps to reinforce and solidify it in your mind. Secondly, your tape or CD puts new portability and power into your informational arsenal. Study or review can take place at virtually any time or location of your choosing.

Last, but not least, stress is reduced as your personal coaching tapes give you greater mastery of your material with each play. Why not try it for yourself?

"IF IT IS TO BE, IT IS UP TO ME. " —ANONYMOUS

Grade Grabber Exercise

(QUICKLY SCAN THIS EXERCISE. JOT DOWN IDEAS, IF
YOU WISH. READ THE NEXT PAGE. WRITE OR ADD TO
YOUR RESPONSES BELOW. GAIN INSIGHT—TAKE ACTION!)

1. What is your greatest challenge in reading Shakespeare?

2. Are there any disadvantages to renting a copy of a
   Shakespearean play from your local video store? Explain.

3. How important is it to read Shakespeare's plays for class?
   List three or four of your reasons.

4. Would you attend a play if it helped you to better understand
   Shakespeare, even though no extra credit was offered? Why?

Watch Hamlet on Your Video Player

But watch out for Hamlet-and-egg productions.

To view video recordings of *Hamlet* or not to view video recordings of *Hamlet*? That is the question for you and for many other students to ponder. William Shakespeare's advice would almost certainly have been "to view" all of his plays, first.

Why? That was the real purpose of his writing. He wrote in order to create a meaningful as well as dramatic experience for the theatergoers of his day. Shakespeare and his audience shared common linguistic and contextual underpinnings. Since you do not, restricting any newly initiated student to the Bard's written script seems rigid and un-Shakespearean.

Your ability to absorb and retain knowledge can be greatly increased by exposure to multi-sensory media. Both research and the experience of many successful students demonstrate this fact. Why not apply it to Shakespeare? Review the following checklist before you begin:

1. Abridged videos may omit key course content.
2. Modern videos may alter plot, locale, characters, etc.
3. Inaccurate video content can sabotage your recollection.
4. Unlike normal television viewing, this does require work.
5. You also need to actively read and review your text.
6. *Complete Dramatic Works of William Shakespeare.* (Libraries can access all 37 plays by Ambrose Video).

All that is required is a modest investment of interest, initiative and care on your part. As a result, you will gain a deeper knowledge and appreciation of William Shakespeare and become a better informed reader of his works.

"THE PLAY'S THE THING."– WILLIAM SHAKESPEARE

Grade Grabber Exercise

(QUICKLY SCAN THIS EXERCISE. JOT DOWN IDEAS, IF
YOU WISH. READ THE NEXT PAGE. WRITE OR ADD TO
YOUR RESPONSES BELOW. GAIN INSIGHT—TAKE ACTION!)

1. Have you ever used your television's closed-captioning
   feature? Did you continue or discontinue using it? Explain.

2. What advantages might closed captioning offer you?

3. What disadvantages might closed captioning offer?

4. Are certain areas of your study routine better suited to closed
   captioning than others? Give a few examples.

Use Closed Captioning

Telecourse technology can help you take better notes.

Colleges frequently offer full-credit video telecourses. Many hearing-impaired students enrolled in these classes make use of a text-activation feature that is built into these videos. Known as "closed captioning," this "CC" technology transmits an immediate, on-screen transcript of a given video program. Many top students have discovered the benefits of adapting it to their own note taking needs, as well.

Video courses vary. Some involve pure "distance learning." Others demand occasional on-campus classes and participation. But one constant remains. Each student is issued a complete set of video recordings, or access to it, along with other prescribed course materials and guidelines.

Because your note taking shifts from a live instructor to a television screen, it appears reasonable for anyone to take advantage of the television's closed-captioning feature.

Using this feature enables you to quickly:

1. Verify the spelling of new names, places or terms.
2. Check the correct spelling of foreign words.
3. Double check a quotation for accuracy.

You can use closed captioning whenever it serves your needs. Some students simply activate it and leave it on. Others find this a distraction and limit on-screen text to "emergency" double-checks.

Use it wisely. Closed captioning is only as reliable as the person who created it. Most are accurate, but not all closed-captioned videos contain verbatim text. Abbreviations, modifications and outright omissions can compromise their value to you as a student. Also make sure that foreign film closed captions match your target language exactly. Make every detail work for you.

"LIFE IS A GREAT BUNDLE OF LITTLE THINGS."
—OLIVER WENDALL HOLMES

Grade Grabber Exercise

(QUICKLY SCAN THIS EXERCISE. JOT DOWN IDEAS, IF YOU WISH. READ THE NEXT PAGE. WRITE OR ADD TO YOUR RESPONSES BELOW. GAIN INSIGHT—TAKE ACTION!)

1. Recall five to ten specific scents that trigger strong, memorable associations in your mind. (Example: Freshly sliced oranges.)

2. Make a similar list of memory triggers using your other senses: taste, touch, sight and sound.

3. When, where and under what circumstances might these cues work best?

4. Target how you might specifically apply this knowledge and optimize your memory under test conditions.

Use Your Brain's Multiple Sensors

There is always room for "Smell-O-Vision." Scented colored markers can offer you a ready harvest of memories.

Would you like to use more of your brain? Studies have shown that your sense of smell can help you do just that. Your mind can remember information more easily if it is linked to a scent (such as lemon) at the time you process, study and/or review information. Many top students use this principle. Why not you?

You can increase your ability to retrieve information whenever you need it by associating a particular name, term, formula, law, principle, topic, etc. in a consistent manner. The only rule you must bear in mind is that the items that "trigger" the best recall are those most distinct from one another in:

1. Color
2. Scent

Many students have found that they do not have to have a lemon slice, for example, for this principle to work. If you are motivated, your unaided mind is quite capable of accomplishing similar results. While colorful scented markers are now available, many students use unscented highlighter pen colors and imagine strong sensory links between knowledge, color and smell with:

- Yellow/Lemon (biting and acidic)
- Blue/Blueberry ("squishy" and juicy)
- Orange/Orange (tangy and pulpy)
- Pink/Watermelon (sticky and sugary)
- Green/Mint (cool and soothing)

"THE MORE ABSTRACT THE TRUTH YOU WISH TO TEACH, THE MORE YOU MUST ALLURE THE SENSES TO IT." —FRIEDRICH NIETZSCHE

Grade Grabber Exercise

(QUICKLY SCAN THIS EXERCISE. JOT DOWN IDEAS, IF YOU WISH. READ THE NEXT PAGE. WRITE OR ADD TO YOUR RESPONSES BELOW. GAIN INSIGHT—TAKE ACTION!)

1. Why do many top students carry note cards?

2. What advantages might note cards have over an information-retrieval device, such as a Personal Digital Assistant (PDA)? Are there disadvantages?

3. Why might you want to carry 5 x 7-inch note cards instead of 3 x 5-inch note cards? When might you choose to use both?

4. Jot down key areas in which note cards can improve student performance. In what subjects might your use of note cards greatly accelerate your ability to learn?

Carry Idea Note Cards or an Idea Notebook

Brilliant ideas and quotations can arrive "out of the blue." Jot them down or lose them forever.

Would you like to discover, develop and present the kind of worthwhile ideas that make instructors reach for their grade books? Reading, lecture notes and study are enormously important. But many top students quickly add that carrying note cards at all times can be an open invitation to — success!

You can maximize the benefits that note cards offer by:

- Always carrying, writing on and reviewing them.
- Exclusively using 5 x 7-inch note cards.
- Writing down ideas and insights immediately.
- Trusting your subconscious mind to serve you.

While most students buy 3 x 5-inch cards, the amount of information you can record on them is limited. In contrast, 5 x 7-inch note cards can be adapted to a wider variety of uses. Large cards offer plenty of room for pasting pictures, maps, charts, graphs, drawings, formulas, etc. The larger card size also makes it less likely that you will misplace or lose them.

The habit of regularly writing down insights and other information can greatly increase your sense of personal organization. The portability of your note cards can stimulate greater purpose, inner directedness and originality. These are the same traits most outstanding students develop. Why not you?

You never know when ideas will arrive "out of the blue." If you note down your ideas consistently, your subconscious mind will do its part to help you succeed. Keep alert, receptive and writing. You will learn that, "If you carry note cards, the ideas will come."

"THE REAL GENIUSES SIMPLY HAVE THEIR BRIGHT IDEAS CLOSER TOGETHER." —GEORG CHRISTOPH LICHTENBERG

Grade Grabber Exercise

(QUICKLY SCAN THIS EXERCISE. JOT DOWN IDEAS, IF YOU WISH. READ THE NEXT PAGE. WRITE OR ADD TO YOUR RESPONSES BELOW. GAIN INSIGHT—TAKE ACTION!)

1. Which subject(s) do you consider the easiest to master?

2. Imagine that you are overloaded with work in your "best" subject. Visualize and then write down two or three possible causes for this difficulty.

3. List any subjects that you find difficult. What might you do to strengthen your abilities and performance levels? Describe two.

Break Down Work into Smaller Steps

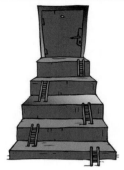

The steps of almost any task automatically adjust to your ability if you master and exploit key details.

Have you ever felt intimidated at the thought of registering for a particular course? Do not feel bad. Many students know that feeling. Even excellent students do. Yet many top students triumph over adversity, often earning better grades than students majoring in the subject. Why? They succeed by frankly admitting their subject "weakness," accepting huge challenges as winnable and being alert to adapting their natural learning style to key course details. Why not do the same?

Consider and then add your own suggestions to the following:

- Get an instructor scouting report from counselors and fellow students. Some instructors have been known to transform fearful students into masterful scholars.
- Limit your full-time semester workload to one super-challenging class. Consider a solo class for a spring or summer session. Seek to reduce stress!
- Buckle down in your reading, note taking and study of critical details. Master rules, laws and formulas.
- Locate additional reading that can better explain the subject—to you. Your college research librarian is an expert who can assist you in transforming difficult material into knowledge. All you need to do is ask!
- Team up with a tutor and/or a sharp study partner.
- Schedule more study time than you think you need.
- Ask your instructor for clarification, as needed.
- Create memorization note cards for subject terms, etc.
- "Overlearn" your subject. Familiarity breeds ease.
- "Model" what top students do to participate in class.

"THE SMALLEST TASK, WELL DONE, BECOMES A MIRACLE OF ACHIEVEMENT." —OG MANDINO

Part 6

Maximize Your Performance with Others

Grade Grabber Exercise

(QUICKLY SCAN THIS EXERCISE. JOT DOWN IDEAS, IF YOU WISH. READ THE NEXT PAGE. WRITE OR ADD TO YOUR RESPONSES BELOW. GAIN INSIGHT—TAKE ACTION!)

1. How might you learn more from your classmates than from your instructor? Are there exceptions? Explain.

2. What sorts of questions are best asked in class? What questions would you ask in a study circle that you might never ask an instructor in a classroom? Explain.

3. What might be your biggest concern, once you are committed to studying with a group of students?

4. What kinds of information might be gained from a study circle that might not otherwise be available alone or with a single study partner? Indicate three or four of these benefits.

Learn More from Colleagues

Their last-minute input can help you out of a jam when nobody else can.

You can ultimately learn more by interacting with your classmates than you can from your instructors. This runs contrary to assumptions about learning held by many students. Yet most instructors would agree—and their experiences confirm—that collaborative learning outside of the classroom can optimize your own academic efforts.

What makes this so? **Time constraints:** Only in an ideal world can instructors offer unlimited one-on-one interaction with students. **Sheer numbers:** Large class sizes restrict instructor availability even more. **Density of subject material:** If you have not heard instructors comment that, "We cannot possibly cover everything we need to cover in class," you will.

Genuine interaction with fellow students outside of the classroom helps to decrease, if not entirely eliminate, classroom inhibitions. This "safe" context serves to quickly end confusion over subject content and gaps in note taking, while clarifying course objectives and approaches. So-called "dumb questions" become acceptable in a friendly, supportive atmosphere of peers.

Sharply defined goals and personal accountability contribute to increased student effectiveness. Openness provides study sessions with potentially livelier discussions. Unexpected creative solutions emerge that can enormously benefit coursework. Good-natured openness creates greater optimism and resilience. Just watch the time fly. Energizing study ideas, test-taking tactics, last-minute pep talks and ongoing support give you a genuine edge.

Get to know your colleagues, make friends with them and make memories, as well. Few college experiences are more satisfying than when your circle of friends initiates a last-minute review session that results in better grades for everyone involved.

"LIFE BEGETS LIFE. ENERGY CREATES ENERGY. IT IS BY SPENDING ONESELF THAT ONE BECOMES RICH." —SARAH BERNHARDT

Grade Grabber Exercise

(QUICKLY SCAN THIS EXERCISE. JOT DOWN IDEAS, IF
YOU WISH. READ THE NEXT PAGE. WRITE OR ADD TO
YOUR RESPONSES BELOW. GAIN INSIGHT—TAKE ACTION!)

1. Are you more likely or less likely to study with an older student?

2. What might be some disadvantages in relating to an older student? Are they based on your experience or mostly on assumptions?

3. In what ways might interacting with an older student prove more mutually beneficial than working with students from your own age group?

4. Do you prefer to let nontraditional students make the first move, or do you prefer to take the initiative? Explain.

Tap an "Open Secret"

Making the grade is easier with non-traditional students in your corner.

Ask virtually any instructor to recall their best students, and the names of numerous nontraditional students will probably fill the list. One reason for their success is that they are more focused and motivated than the norm. Nontraditional students are, quite possibly, the greatest "open secret" to success that you will encounter on campus. Get to know them.

A great deal of their commitment to excellence has been crystallized by life experiences, both good and bad, and by a quest for personal and professional growth. Add mature insightfulness into the equation, and you will quickly begin to appreciate what makes this group a hands-down choice for students in the know.

The advantages nontraditional students offer you include:

1. Disinterest in your love life.
2. Disinterest in hearing about your family's problems.
3. Patience, friendliness, respectfulness and support.
4. Thorough preparation for classes, groups and studying.
5. Purpose-driven approach.
6. More seasoned critical-thinking skills.
7. Treat you as a colleague, regardless of your age.
8. Feel a vested team interest in your success.
9. Willing to locate and to share findings helpful to you.
10. Will share tips that can help you to succeed.
11. Always on time for you.
12. Offer a stable sounding board for ideas or concerns.

If you are truly serious about making better grades, tap into this group. It is probably the biggest "open secret" on campus. But you still need to seize the opportunity to capitalize on it.

"MANY OPPORTUNITIES ARE LOST FOR WANT OF ASKING."
—PROVERB

Grade Grabber Exercise

(QUICKLY SCAN THIS EXERCISE. JOT DOWN IDEAS, IF
YOU WISH. READ THE NEXT PAGE. WRITE OR ADD TO
YOUR RESPONSES BELOW. GAIN INSIGHT—TAKE ACTION!)

1. How might a study partner benefit you?

2. When a classmate calls you with an "emergency," how do
   you decide whether or not that person's concern is worthy of
   your time?

3. In contrast to the above-noted student, what kind of help are
   you prepared to give to a study partner?

4. What would be your biggest reason for dropping a study
   partner?

Demonstrate Reliability

This does not include "emergency" support for unreliable colleagues.

Genuine academic networking requires much more than a mechanical scribbling down of names and contact information. It implies a reasonably coherent, active and ongoing study partnership. Above all, it demands reliability.

In order to be successful, both you and your prospective study partner should be willing to promote the following:

1. Mutual respect and support.
2. Regular attendance (absences offer "zero" benefits).
3. Good note-taking skills.
4. Reliable study habits.
5. Honesty.
6. Availability via e-mail, phone, etc. (within bounds).
7. Accountability.
8. Active, two-way communication.
9. Availability for study and review.
10. Willingness to go the extra mile, if necessary.

Too many students routinely choose to procrastinate, cut class and otherwise sabotage their own academic progress, while ignoring the consequences of these choices. This complacent attitude inevitably leads to disaster. You need to keep students who are a liability at arm's length.

Personal reliability is the first step in building a strong network. The second step lies in intelligently selecting a study partner. The final step is in knowing when to go it alone.

"THE WORLD IS MOVING AT AN ACCELERATING CLIP AND HAS WANING PATIENCE FOR PEOPLE WHO CHOOSE NOT TO KEEP UP."
—DOUG SMART

Grade Grabber Exercise

(QUICKLY SCAN THIS EXERCISE. JOT DOWN IDEAS, IF
YOU WISH. READ THE NEXT PAGE. WRITE OR ADD TO
YOUR RESPONSES BELOW. GAIN INSIGHT—TAKE ACTION!)

1. What do you think causes writer's block?

2. What steps do you normally take to overcome writer's block?
   Describe.

3. How can expressing frustration be a key to renewed writing?

4. In what way can sight, sound and course materials get you
   back to writing quickly and confidently?

Rage on the Page

Jumpstart your rough draft like a "writing tornado." Once the words flow, simply focus on what you know.

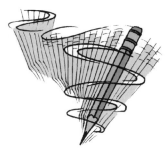

Maybe you have experienced "writer's block" at one time or another. If so, you know how it can rob you of time and energy. Many of the best students know how to bypass writer's block and get back to writing like a raging whirlwind—like a writing tornado. The good news is that you can, too.

You have heard that the pen is mightier than the sword. But once writer's block takes root, the tongue becomes even mightier than the pen. Your own experience can verify this.

Talk! The first impulse many students have is to share their frustration with someone else. Often the simple act of speaking to someone who is willing to listen and to ask follow-up questions is enough to eliminate writer's block. **Audio record** your conversation with your friend's permission. Not only will your friend be even more willing to help, but your project will be taken much more seriously.

Write, now! After your conversation, your fresh insights and renewed motivation may be enough to keep your ideas flowing and get you back on track. In addition to any notes that you may have jotted down, you can always refer back to the recording to word process any or all useful information. This may be all you need.

"Rage on the page," if needed. Write down your brainstorm of key ideas as you re-listen to your audio recording and actively review course materials, etc. Keep raging and keep writing. Each newly written brainstorm entry has the potential to bring your paper to new life and your thinking to new heights, while reducing writer's block to dust in your mind's rear-view mirror.

"WORDS ON A PAGE ASSUME A TANGIBLE REALITY. THIS TANGIBLE REALITY HAS UNMISTAKABLE POWER BECAUSE IT DOESN'T LIMIT—IT ONLY EXPANDS." —MICHAEL YOUNG

Grade Grabber Exercise

(QUICKLY SCAN THIS EXERCISE. JOT DOWN IDEAS, IF YOU WISH. READ THE NEXT PAGE. WRITE OR ADD TO YOUR RESPONSES BELOW. GAIN INSIGHT—TAKE ACTION!)

1. List some practical reasons for having your written work proofread by certain people and not others.

2. What should you look for when proofreading another student's paper?

3. How might a proofreader sharpen your learning skills?

4. How might you react if a proofreader points out a number of flaws in your work?

Evaluate Your Proofreader

Never turn important feedback into a kissing contest.

Be honest. No matter how studious you are, getting top grades demands that someone proofreads your paperwork. But that does not literally mean that virtually anyone is qualified to do so.

You might ask, "Couldn't I just ask that cute student I invited out for dinner to proofread my paper before we eat?"

You could, but that would be a big mistake. Proofreading is a critically important step that can help ensure success. Errors in punctuation, spelling, logical flow, formatting, citations, etc. can be easily overlooked, especially when assignments start piling up higher than the Parthenon. Errors you might never catch will jump from the page when read by someone with a fresh, critical perspective. If the proofreader is careless, you lose.

Selecting a reader who has your best interests "at heart" is not enough. Proofreading often requires the steely discipline that will risk making you uncomfortable now, so you won't be later. The criteria found in a good proofreader include the ability to:

1. Read and work through your paper thoroughly.
2. Critically assess it as a whole and in detail.
3. Point out what might make it a better paper.

Be honest, reasonable and realistic. Find the right person to do your proofreading for you, and keep all pressing academic business and romantic activities separate.

Dates do not want to proofread for you. They only want to be liked. If the truth were told, they would rather eat meatloaf than proofread your take-home exam. Truthfully, wouldn't you?

"ONE ARROW DOES NOT BRING DOWN TWO BIRDS."
— TURKISH PROVERB

Grade Grabber Exercise

(QUICKLY SCAN THIS EXERCISE. JOT DOWN IDEAS, IF
YOU WISH. READ THE NEXT PAGE. WRITE OR ADD TO
YOUR RESPONSES BELOW. GAIN INSIGHT—TAKE ACTION!)

1. How likely are you to reach a decision? Do you tend to follow your own thinking or do you consult others? Give an example.

2. Is finding "the one-and-best decision" possible? Explain.

3. List some key factors that contribute to better decisions. Do any items on your list change when applied to work groups? How?

4. In what way can hasty or slow decisions undermine the quality of an important group project?

Keep Simple Decisions Simple

Avoid complicating matters. A clearer answer is often at your fingertips.

Would you like to arrive at better decisions more quickly? Many mediocre students end up missing the proverbial forest for the trees. The bad news is that you may be teamed with them in a class. But, like most top students, you need not allow them to delay or otherwise compromise your decision making—and your grades.

The following four considerations can optimize your decision making. First, consider the folly of striving to find the **best decision**. In reality, the best solution—like perfection itself—is an elusive ideal . . . an impossible dream.

The second approach seeks out **better decisions**. Selecting one or several better solutions from among your research findings can reward you with reduced stress. It can also ensure more manageable and satisfying results. Striving for better decisions makes learning much more interesting and dynamic, since it encourages the possibility of even greater discoveries and breakthroughs.

Third, **hastily reached decisions** should always be avoided. Pressures that contribute to such impulsiveness are often tied to time, intimidation, fear, guilt, fatigue and student impatience. Nevertheless, the quality of your decisions can be greatly improved by allowing yourself adequate time to gather and weigh information prior to reaching any conclusions.

Fourth, mediocre students often turn a **50/50 decision** into a big time waster by insisting on the need for more data, even when time is running short. Searching for more information when plenty of facts are already staring you in the face can cause unnecessary stress and undermine the efforts of all members of the group. If you are presented with two equally viable paths, a simple coin toss can settle things.

"MAKE EVERYTHING AS SIMPLE AS POSSIBLE, BUT NOT SIMPLER."
—ALBERT EINSTEIN

Part 7

Prepare for Tests without Distress

Grade Grabber Exercise

(QUICKLY SCAN THIS EXERCISE. JOT DOWN IDEAS, IF YOU WISH. READ THE NEXT PAGE. WRITE OR ADD TO YOUR RESPONSES BELOW. GAIN INSIGHT—TAKE ACTION!)

1. What added benefits can result when you rehearse as well as study for an exam?

2. Does it matter where you sit when preparing for an exam?

3. What sort of attitude or activities can optimize rehearsal work?

4. How might time considerations or the presence of colleagues help or hinder your exam preparation? Explain.

Rehearse for a Winning Exam

Onsite preparation builds confidence and mastery.

Have you ever experienced anxiety just before a major exam? Virtually every student has. Yet, many exceptional students have discovered a great way to harness anxiety in their favor. Instead of focusing on negative outcomes, they rehearse positive results.

Here are a couple of suggestions for doing just that:

1. **Vividly imagine yourself inside the classroom** on exam day. You can do this repeatedly over several days for greater confidence and mastery. It is easy. It is portable. Engage all of your senses as you actively review important information. Mentally rehearse "seeing" yourself responding correctly to every exam question.

2. **Physically visit the exam room** when it is not otherwise in use. If your classroom is unavailable during weekdays, see if it is available during weeknight or weekend hours. (If an in-class rehearsal cannot be arranged, simply revert to the previous suggestion noted above.)

    When you arrive for your exam rehearsal, sit in the same seat you will occupy on exam day. This is your "success zone." You will find that this simple detail can make a huge difference in your thinking on exam day.

    Seriously study, review and reabsorb your material using your books, notes, handouts, etc. Do the sort of "scripted" exam rehearsal that will enable you to have your exam content down cold. Even if you have study partners present, rehearsing should be done in a relaxed, focused and unhurried atmosphere. Experience a sense of confident preparation and mastery. Such a memory can propel you toward remarkable success on exam day.

"THE POOREST EXPERIENCE IS RICH ENOUGH FOR ALL THE PURPOSES OF EXPRESSING THOUGHT." —RALPH WALDO EMERSON

Grade Grabber Exercise

(QUICKLY SCAN THIS EXERCISE. JOT DOWN IDEAS, IF YOU WISH. READ THE NEXT PAGE. WRITE OR ADD TO YOUR RESPONSES BELOW. GAIN INSIGHT—TAKE ACTION!)

1. Are you an "early bird" or a "night owl"? What are the advantages and disadvantages of your personal sleep cycle?

2. What is your attitude about deadlines, once time and energy are fast running out? Explain.

3. How might a top student who is normally an excellent time manager suddenly find herself behind schedule and working late into the night?

4. What are some ideas that you or your classmates have used to keep studying late into the night? What worked? What did not?

Set Your Alarm Clock

Meet deadlines with humor and creativity.

When are you most mentally alert and productive? If you are a "night owl," your best writing, brainstorming and study take place late at night. You see putting a completed project to bed first as the key to eventually drifting off to sleep.

Naturally, things are different if you are an "early bird." Early birds are first out of bed ready to "wake up the chickens." If you greet each new day with a mind so percolating with eye-opening ideas, observations and energy that your face should be on a jar of *Taster's Choice*® coffee, you are an early bird.

It can be a rude awakening for collegiate night owls and early birds to accommodate new semester schedules, unforeseen family emergencies or multiple course deadlines. While your personal medical needs, stamina and good judgment should overrule any other considerations, it is interesting (and amusing) to discover what some students do to keep focused, productive and on task.

Staying on your feet: Emergency room doctors routinely stay awake by remaining on their feet. Building on this idea, some students use a bedroom dresser top as a desk. Others swear that chewing **bubble gum** keeps their minds alert and focused. Still other wide-eyed students reduce bathroom visits by snacking on **chocolate-covered coffee beans**. Many educators and students recommend **Mozart music** for improved study, focus and recall.

The two wind-up alarm clocks method: One alarm is placed by your night stand. The second is posted fourteen feet from your bed and set fifteen minutes later than the first clock. This can eliminate a crisis resulting from oversleeping or a power failure.

The water-clock method mobilizes an 8-ounce glass of water — a sort of bio-clock "set to go off" in four hours, más o menos! As to the question of whether this is an anal-retentive or an anal-expulsive measure, "Neither!" is the correct answer.

"THREE O'CLOCK IS ALWAYS TOO LATE OR TOO EARLY FOR WHAT YOU WANT TO DO." —JEAN-PAUL SARTRE

Grade Grabber Exercise

(QUICKLY SCAN THIS EXERCISE. JOT DOWN IDEAS, IF YOU WISH. READ THE NEXT PAGE. WRITE OR ADD TO YOUR RESPONSES BELOW. GAIN INSIGHT—TAKE ACTION!)

1. Take a moment to list a few sources of stress in your life. (Example: Waiting in line.)

2. What is your biggest source of stress? (Circle one from above.)

3. Vividly imagine what it would feel like to magically dissolve your biggest stressor—every time! What words might you use to describe your experience? (Example: Energized.)

4. Picture someone you know who embodies most, if not all, of your responses to #3. Consistent with that person's example, write down and commit to one behavioral change you want in your life.

Observe, Relax, React

Three easy steps that melt stress away like magic.

Test stress can compromise the best-prepared student. If you have ever been unable to remember important information during a test, yet could instantly do so in the hallway afterward, listen up! You can defeat stress, if you choose.

Even the best of students experience stress, if not flat-out panic, from time to time. What separates better students from the rest is their ability to process stress in a way that does not compromise performance. If you have ever wondered at their ability to breeze through their work, know that you can be just as successful at neutralizing stress.

Stress is a reaction, not a battle plan. To defeat stress, follow this three-step method and maximize your performance in any situation. Here is your battle plan:

- Observe
- Relax
- React

Observe: Let a little time pass. Take a couple of deep breaths, if that is helpful to you. Quietly observe. This quiet observation will expand your ability to think clearly. **Relax:** Simply allow yourself to enter into the meaning of this word. Give yourself permission to relax; be present within the moment. Relaxation prepares you to react more powerfully to the task at hand. **React:** Even if you must work quickly, "make haste slowly." Stay poised and on target.

You can repeat this three-step method anytime you feel the need to melt away stress. By using this simple battle plan, you can be much more focused, articulate and on target. You can succeed!

"A GENIUS IS ONE WHO SHOOTS AT SOMETHING NO ONE CAN SEE— AND HITS IT." —ANONYMOUS

Grade Grabber Exercise

(QUICKLY SCAN THIS EXERCISE. JOT DOWN IDEAS, IF YOU WISH. READ THE NEXT PAGE. WRITE OR ADD TO YOUR RESPONSES BELOW. GAIN INSIGHT—TAKE ACTION!)

1. Which students are normally first to leave the exam room? Explain.

2. Do top students ever leave the exam room last? Explain.

3. What is your biggest enemy during an exam? (Examples: Content, the clock, etc.) What can you do to perform better?

4. What is a good way to make exam details work for you?

Make Haste, Slowly

Savvy students center their efforts on balancing speed with accuracy.

Have you ever noticed the first thing some students do once their exams are completed? They leave! If you are among many students who witness this, you may feel a bit intimidated. After all, they "aced" the exam, right? Not necessarily!

Contrary to popular notions about early departures, instructors realize that students who are the first to leave an exam usually do so because they have done poorly. They are generally unprepared, unmotivated or careless. How different it is for those who score well.

Savvy students perform consistently on exams because they:

- Get needed rest, arrive early and strive to remain sharp.
- Plan on exploiting every minute of exam time.
- Keep material fresh by reviewing it alone, as well as with a study partner.
- Wisely estimate time requirements for different questions: multiple choice, fill in the blank, true or false, etc.
- Have strong openings planned for blue book questions.
- Take the time to jot down a rough outline. Then begin.
- Double check all work when extra time is available.

There is little that anyone can expect from disinterested or "inert" individuals. But unintentionally careless students can take quick and necessary steps to change. Whether you are a top student or one who aspires to be one, speed and accuracy should be continually balanced to maximize your exam performance.

Be careful! When you focus too much on content, you can lose the battle against the clock, leaving gaps in your work. On the other hand, working so fast that you are blind to vital details is deadly, too. Work quickly, but do not rush. Make haste, slowly.

"The haste of a fool is the slowest thing in the world."
—Thomas Shadwell

Watch Out for Key Essay Words

Knowing specific essay question terms can trigger better answers.

Analyze: Target the most important ideas. Indicate why they are important and show how they are interrelated.

Argue: Promote a specific position by providing strong evidence, both pro and con, that ultimately serve to support your conclusion.

Comment: Offer a brief, strong and perceptive discussion based upon what you have learned, understand and know to be true or untrue.

Compare: Stress the similarities, but reveal your understanding of the differences.

Contrast: Stress the differences.

Critique: Weigh the pros and cons in detail. Supply your personal opinion based on available evidence, noting its completeness or limitations.

Define: Provide the simplest, "bare bones" meaning.

Demonstrate: Give your opinion, assessment or conclusion, and show how it is supported by the evidence.

Describe: Provide vividly detailed information.

Diagram: Draw and provide labels for a chart, graph, etc.

Discuss: Present both sides of an issue or topic, at length and in detail.

Enumerate: List and number important points.

Evaluate: Present pros and cons with your observations and judgments.

Explain: Provide reasons for an incident or circumstance.

Illustrate: Provide a clear example.

Interpret: Reformulate and communicate the same meaning in a simpler manner.

Justify: Support your ideas with convincing evidence and well-reasoned argumentation.

List: Provide items in a list without details or numbering. (*See* **Enumerate.**)

Outline: Make a brief structural sketch of main subject ideas that include topic headings and subheadings.

Prove: Provide evidence and justification in your response.

Relate: Provide logical interconnections in your response.

Review: Summarize the most essential content.

State: Provide an itemized list of main points, without going into detail about those points.

Summarize: Briefly and perceptively highlight and present each of the main points.

Support: Provide strong evidence to back up each claim.

Trace: Provide the complete steps or chain of events requested.

"SOMETIMES QUESTIONS ARE MORE IMPORTANT THAN ANSWERS."
—NANCY WILLARD

Grade Grabber Exercise

(QUICKLY SCAN THIS EXERCISE. JOT DOWN IDEAS, IF
YOU WISH. READ THE NEXT PAGE. WRITE OR ADD TO
YOUR RESPONSES BELOW. GAIN INSIGHT—TAKE ACTION!)

1. How is academic writing different from other kinds of writing?

2. Why are numerous footnotes alone not enough to earn you a top grade?

3. What are some characteristics of a well-written paper?

4. Why do you think instructors find a well-researched and well-written paper demands less time to grade than a poor one?

Stay on Target as You Write

You do not need to reinvent the wheel, but you do need to refer back to it if your paper is about wheels.

There is an old saying that probably originated in sports – or warfare: "Hit them. Hit them hard. Hit them often!" How does this apply to writing? Vigorous, compelling and content-driven writing is not enough. It must be logical, polished and focused.

Here is a deceptively simple "Three H" approach to simplify the writing process, while vastly increasing your paper's quality and clarity in the eyes of your instructors.

1. **Hit them**: Clearly and promptly open your paper by stating what it is about.
2. **Hit them hard**: Provide your best research findings. This is your chance to really impress your instructor that you have, within the guidelines given to you, done your best to assess both sides of the issue before formulating your paper's contention.
3. **Hit them often.** Regularly refer back to your paper's main contention as you write.

Be forewarned about relying too much on a good thing. To constantly refer back to your main point is almost as bad as to make no reference to it at all.

It helps to have someone else read your paper. In fact, many instructors are more than willing to read your rough draft. Ready assistance is also available at your college's writing lab. Why not take advantage of every opportunity to refine your paper? It pays!

Well-written papers put all of the pieces of the puzzle together, do it in an intelligent and well-organized manner and are the easiest to grade. Why not eliminate all of the guesswork on your instructor's part? After all, no one wants to reinvent the wheel.

"LEARN AS MUCH BY WRITING AS BY READING." —LORD ACTON

Grade Grabber Exercise

(QUICKLY SCAN THIS EXERCISE. JOT DOWN IDEAS, IF YOU WISH. READ THE NEXT PAGE. WRITE OR ADD TO YOUR RESPONSES BELOW. GAIN INSIGHT—TAKE ACTION!)

1. How is studying for a blue book exam different from a fill-in-the-blank or multiple-choice exam? Give examples.

2. Jim tells you that a great way to write a blue book exam is to "pad" your essays with key terms. What is wrong with that approach?

3. How is making up your own questions helpful in preparing for a blue book exam?

Furnish Your Blue Book with Needed Details

Vital essay elements help keep your house in order.

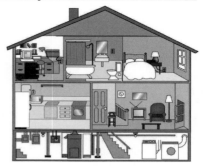

Maximizing the impact of your blue book essay response is a lot like building your dream home. Details make the difference.

Let us say that you hired a contractor to build your dream home. You would expect this person to make a detailed assessment of all critical information, including your specific requirements and guidelines. Construction would then conform to those details.

However, how would you grade the results of a builder who consistently ignored most, if not all, of the information, needs and guidelines that you provided? Would it be reasonable to award a bonus to such a builder for completing the job ahead of schedule?

Instructors feel the same way whenever important details are omitted from blue book exams. Whenever you give them what they need, it is easier to earn a grade "that you can both live with."

Consider the following suggestions:

- Review and memorize important readings, lecture notes, handouts, etc. and practice a few introductory and closing sentence ideas. This will help to keep your essay focused.
- Adopt a plan of attack. Think up and then rehearse possible exam questions and responses.
- Consistently include key terms in your essay in ways that reveal both understanding and mastery.
- Write clear, concise and unhurried essays. These communicate care, intelligence and attention to detail. This is how many top students excel.
- View each essay exam as the chance to build your academic reputation, to refine your writing skills and to "teach" your instructor what you know.

"TO TEACH IS TO LEARN TWICE." —JOSEPH JOUBERT

Part 8

Unlock Secrets at Your Campus Library

Grade Grabber Exercise

(QUICKLY SCAN THIS EXERCISE. JOT DOWN IDEAS, IF YOU WISH. READ THE NEXT PAGE. WRITE OR ADD TO YOUR RESPONSES BELOW. GAIN INSIGHT—TAKE ACTION!)

1. Why do colleges and universities provide academic libraries on campus when plenty of municipal libraries are available?

2. How is using an internet database inferior to exploiting your college library's resources?

3. What is the one thing that sharp students do to obtain the most help from library personnel?

4. Why do many top students and scholarly professionals regard the role of the research librarian as an academically vital one?

Start Bookmarking Your College Library's Web Pages

Consulting research librarians, academic databases, etc. can take your work to the next level.

Why should you take advantage of your **college library**? As an "academic" library, its personnel, databases and other premium informational resources are uniquely positioned to help you take your work to the next level. The rest is up to you.

Even modest efforts can result in enormous personal gains, if you are willing to get out of your own way and ask for assistance from a research librarian. That is precisely how many formerly "mediocre" students became outstanding students. You can, too.

Why are non-campus research approaches less desirable?

Internet surfing, for all of its convenience, is often weighed down by millions of "hits." At worst, surfing provides content of uneven or questionable value. At best, it lacks the complete range of authoritative information available at your college library.

Public libraries are geared towards the reading demands of the general public. Professional staffing aside, these collections cannot compete with your college library's academic resources.

Know that your college's library personnel are eager to serve you, but you must arrive prepared. Visit the college library's main web page, so you have a good idea of what resources are available to you. Present your research librarian with the assignment sheet that your instructor gave you. Be positive and take good notes.

Research librarians represent an enormous asset. Pick up any scholarly book. More likely than not, you will find the names of several research librarians in the "Acknowledgements" section.

If increasing your grade point average and strengthening your overall academic skills are important to you, get to know your college research librarian! Make your first visit one of many.

"KNOW THINE OPPORTUNITY." —PITTACUS

Grade Grabber Exercise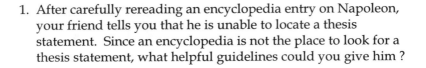
(QUICKLY SCAN THIS EXERCISE. JOT DOWN IDEAS, IF
YOU WISH. READ THE NEXT PAGE. WRITE OR ADD TO
YOUR RESPONSES BELOW. GAIN INSIGHT—TAKE ACTION!)

1. After carefully rereading an encyclopedia entry on Napoleon,
   your friend tells you that he is unable to locate a thesis
   statement. Since an encyclopedia is not the place to look for a
   thesis statement, what helpful guidelines could you give him ?

2. Sue decides to ignore the introduction of the book she is
   reading for class. How might she later regret doing this?

3. Charlie tells you that he has located a solid book containing an
   eight-sentence thesis statement. Is he right? Explain.

Pinpoint Thesis Statements Like a Pro

Why airport books on Napoleon never fly in academe.

Critical reading assignments are regularly included in history courses. Sometimes students may select a book of their choice. Very often, they must choose from a list of approved books.

Would you like to know what savvy students accomplish through the power of the thesis statement? First, they use the thesis statement to quickly pinpoint their reading focus. Next, they rely on it to provide an easy writing template to classify and arrange notes that make writing response papers easier.

How can you identify a thesis statement? Consider the following criteria:

- **Introduction Chapter** (No introduction? Forget the book!)
- **Argument** or Contention
- **One- or two-sentence statement** maximum

As noted above, the thesis statement is the author's argument about a topic. A one-sentence example might be: *"Napoleon Bonaparte was a traitor to the French Republic."*

A two-sentence thesis statement is not always uninterrupted. Note the break in this example: *"Napoleon was the greatest hero in the history of the French Republic. Many have heard stories of his life. Without Napoleon as his example, Charles De Gaulle could not have ended the German Occupation of France in World War II."*

By the way, the only thing worse than the lack of a thesis statement is a string of "arguments" posing as a thesis statement. Such ploys are nothing more than rants — not the real article.

"MANY BOOKS REQUIRE NO THOUGHT FROM THOSE WHO READ THEM, AND FOR A VERY SIMPLE REASON; THEY MADE NO SUCH DEMAND UPON THOSE WHO WROTE THEM." —CHARLES CALEB COLTON

Grade Grabber Exercise

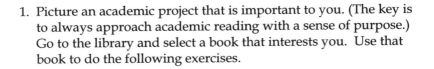

(QUICKLY SCAN THIS EXERCISE. JOT DOWN IDEAS, IF
YOU WISH. READ THE NEXT PAGE. WRITE OR ADD TO
YOUR RESPONSES BELOW. GAIN INSIGHT—TAKE ACTION!)

1. Picture an academic project that is important to you. (The key is to always approach academic reading with a sense of purpose.) Go to the library and select a book that interests you. Use that book to do the following exercises.

2. Using the form* on the opposite page, indicate the author, title, publisher information and the library call number.

3. Take three or four minutes to scan the book's table of contents, introduction, index, random chapters and the conclusion. Rate and be sure to include comments as to the value of your book for an academic project.

4. Once completed, compare your bibliography notes with what appears on the following two pages.

*You will find a set of forms in the Appendix of this book.

BIBLIOGRAPHY FILE

AUTHOR-

TITLE-   [   ]

CITY: PUBLISHER, DATE-

LIBRARY & LOCATION	CALL NUMBER

RATE THIS TITLE: 1 2 3 4 5

COMMENTS-

ASK!!! YOU MAY BE CLOSER TO A BREAKTHROUGH THAN YOU REALIZE.
YOUR RESEARCH LIBRARIAN KNOWS HOW TO GET YOU THERE—FAST!

BIBLIOGRAPHY FILE

AUTHOR- *Rowland, Thomas J.*

TITLE- *George B. McClellan and Civil War History: In the Shadow of Grant and Sherman.*   [*Book*]

CITY: PUBLISHER, DATE- *Kent, OH: Kent State University Press, 1998.*

LIBRARY & LOCATION	CALL NUMBER
University of Wisconsin (Madison)	*E467.1.M2 R69 1998*

RATE THIS TITLE: 1   2   3   4   (5)

COMMENTS-

My course instructor wants more "contrast" information in my second draft on General McClellan. This study is pure gold. Rowland challenges many accepted views regarding George B. McClellan as excessively antagonistic and inconsistent with historical record. This book offers solid contrasting information to the methods and conclusions of two other Civil War historians that I read for this paper: Stephen Sears and Bruce Catton.

ASK!!! YOU MAY BE CLOSER TO A BREAKTHROUGH THAN YOU REALIZE. YOUR RESEARCH LIBRARIAN KNOWS HOW TO GET YOU THERE—FAST!

BIBLIOGRAPHY FILE

AUTHOR- *Rowland, Thomas J.*

> IT IS IMPORTANT TO INDICATE
> THE WORK'S <u>FORMAT</u>, TOO.

TITLE- *George B. McClellan and Civil War History: In the Shadow of Grant and Sherman.* [Book]

> MANY TOP STUDENTS USE MORE THAN ONE LIBRARY. RESEARCH
> OFTEN INCLUDES INTERLIBRARY LOANS. KNOW WHERE TO LOOK.

CITY: PUBLISHER, DATE- *Kent, OH: Kent State University Press, 1998.*

> LIBRARY OF CONGRESS (SHOWN HERE) OR
> DEWEY DECIMAL CALL NUMBER.

LIBRARY & LOCATION	CALL NUMBER
University of Wisconsin (Madison)	*E467.1.M2 R69 1998*

> CIRCLE A NUMBER ON YOUR OWN RATING SCALE:
> 1 = AWFUL...5 = AWESOME!

RATE THIS TITLE: 1   2   3   4   (5)

> INCLUDE USEFUL COMMENTS. YOUR NEEDS CAN CHANGE.
> NOTE SPECIFIC REASONS FOR YOUR RATING.

COMMENTS-

My course instructor wants more "contrast" information in my second draft on General McClellan. This study is pure gold. Rowland challenges many accepted views regarding George B. McClellan as excessively antagonistic and inconsistent with historical record. This book offers solid contrasting information to the methods and conclusions of two other Civil War historians that I read for this paper: Stephen Sears and Bruce Catton.

ASK!!! YOU MAY BE CLOSER TO A BREAKTHROUGH THAN YOU REALIZE. YOUR RESEARCH LIBRARIAN KNOWS HOW TO GET YOU THERE—FAST!

Grade Grabber Exercise

(QUICKLY SCAN THIS EXERCISE. JOT DOWN IDEAS, IF YOU WISH. READ THE NEXT PAGE. WRITE OR ADD TO YOUR RESPONSES BELOW. GAIN INSIGHT—TAKE ACTION!)

1. Your instructors place a great deal of emphasis on accuracy. Why do you think this is so important to them?

2. Students often "go over" their work at the last minute. What do you think top students do differently than mediocre ones?

3. What five or six things could cause you to incorrectly record information?

4. What might help you to improve the accuracy of your work in the future? (Examples: printing clearly, taking your time, etc.)

Get Details to Work for You

Forget eyestrain. Creating a "page layout box" can speed your ability to find passages.

Imagine that you are gearing up for an important research paper deadline. Time is running short and attending to last-minute details is critical. Heading your list of key concerns is this one from your course syllabus: "Your instructor will spot check all research papers for accuracy. Careless submissions will be marked down—No exceptions."

While research papers are an inevitable part of academic life, you can greatly increase the quality of your work as well as your ability to verify your original notes—even at the last minute. One suggestion you may find useful is to add your own "page layout box" to your research note cards. Like cogs in a gear, your page layout boxes can add speed, accuracy and power to any reference work. They can reduce stress, eyestrain and fatigue.

One top student created the following page layout box to save time resifting through a densely written academic journal. The "box" targets page 987 of the original text. Simple plot lines graphically pinpoint where the quotation can be found.

This simple and effective time saver promotes accuracy. Try it.
1. Draw the outline of a page somewhere on your note card.
2. Use a pen or pencil to plot lines that pinpoint passages.
3. Mark the page number inside the page layout box.

"TO KEEP EVERY COG AND WHEEL IS THE FIRST PRECAUTION OF INTELLIGENT TINKERING." —ALDO LEOPOLD

Grade Grabber Exercise

(QUICKLY SCAN THIS EXERCISE. JOT DOWN IDEAS, IF
YOU WISH. READ THE NEXT PAGE. WRITE OR ADD TO
YOUR RESPONSES BELOW. GAIN INSIGHT—TAKE ACTION!)

1. What steps can you take to increase your chances for a top research project grade?

2. Who can offer you the best assistance when your research gets bogged down?

3. Excluding stress, list four or five reasons why it is not a good idea to read and then write your research paper in one day.

4. What can you do to encourage your mind to generate more useful and insightful research writing?

Be Attentive to Emerging Impact

Let your mind soar. Even brief studies can bring unexpected and profound awareness.

Some contemporary observers claim that today you are exposed to as much information in one year as your great-grandparents experienced in a lifetime. One thing seems certain. Nobody expects an information slowdown, but some students are better prepared.

Regardless of whether you are required to submit a briefly "sketched" research study or a more detailed report, you can take steps to increase your chances for a better grade. Here is how:

1. Research, read and thoughtfully record information.
2. Deliberately allow the material incubation time.
3. Return to your notes to develop any emerging themes.
4. **Select and write about your best ideas and insights.**

First: Research and/or read and record information. Actively seek out, note down and follow up useful themes, quotations, observations, consistencies, contradictions, etc. Take control, right here. If you need advice as to where to look, ask your instructor, a research librarian or a smart colleague or friend. **Second**: Deliberately allow the material incubation time. Your brain needs the break and your subconscious mind is ready to go to work. Your mind can soar if you give it the time it needs to work its magic for you. **Third**: Actively review your notes, looking for emerging ideas and flashes of insight. Do this repeatedly. Done well, you can approach your next step with increasing confidence. **Fourth**: Write your paper. Be bright. Be insightful. Be original. Aside from your grade, strong research work can make you proud of your successes, while inspiring you to build on them.

"IT WAS AS THOUGH SOMETHING UNEXPECTED JUST GOT UP, LOOKED ME RIGHT IN THE EYE AND SAID, 'HELLO!'" —ANONYMOUS

Grade Grabber Exercise

(QUICKLY SCAN THIS EXERCISE. JOT DOWN IDEAS, IF
YOU WISH. READ THE NEXT PAGE. HOW CAN WRITING A
BOOK REVIEW SHARPEN THINKING? GAIN INSIGHT—TAKE ACTION!)

Regardless of the course, your instructor and/or research librarian
can provide invaluable book review advice and examples. Ask!
Consider the following points for writing a history book review.
How might you adapt them for use in other humanities classes?

State the name, title and/or qualifications of the author.
What is the book about?
What is the main argument of the book?
What resources are used?

> Primary (Original)
> Oral
> Survey
> Newly discovered manuscript
> Archival
> Secondary (Texts based on primary sources)
> Other

What issues does the author voice?

> Positive
> Negative
> Open
> Biased

What are your reactions?

> Structural advantages or problems
> Research advantages or limitations
> Validity of conclusions

Do you recommend this book?

> Why? / Why not?
> Is there one or several reading audiences to
> consider in making your recommendation?

What questions does the book leave unanswered?

> Intentional / Unintentional / Unavoidable
> Expected / Unexpected
> Acceptable / Unacceptable

Write a Review
Do a book report instead of a book review and you lose.

A lot of new college students wrongly assume that a book report is identical to a book review. Worse still, some intentionally submit a book report for a book review assignment. WARNING: "Getting it wrong" can result in meager, if any, grade points. Why would you invite failure?

Kim Anderson almost always earned top grades for her high school book reports. Imagine her horror when she spotted a "D" on her first college paper. Upset? Kim felt so bad that she waited until she got home to read her professor's comments.

Her professor wrote: "This would merit a top grade if I had asked for a book report. You introduced the author well and wrote a perceptive narrative on the book. I was also pleased to read what you learned about the subject and how much it shed new light on this course. You included some fine quotations, too. But I wanted a **book REVIEW! Unlike a book report, a book review must isolate and discuss the most important ideas, viewpoints and insights of the book under discussion.** Assessing the author's background, the context and the main theme and supporting arguments of the book are key. A brief summary, not a rehashing of the entire book, is all that a book review requires. Direct quotations should be brief and used only when necessary. **In contrast to a book report, a book review offers you the opportunity to take a probing, analytical and provocative (i.e. non-inflammatory) approach.**

"**Would you recommend this book? Be fair**. Whatever your answer, your reader needs plenty of solidly convincing reasons to **support** your arguments, including **your personal reactions, questions and insights.** That is why your book report fell well short of the mark. It cost you in grade points. Learn from this."

After meeting with her instructor and an on-campus research librarian, Kim created a checklist for writing future reviews. Kim learned, worked smarter and scored well on her next book review.

"ONE CANNOT REVIEW A BAD BOOK WITHOUT SHOWING OFF."
—W.H. AUDEN

Grade Grabber Exercise

(QUICKLY SCAN THIS EXERCISE. JOT DOWN IDEAS, IF YOU WISH. READ THE NEXT PAGE. WRITE OR ADD TO YOUR RESPONSES BELOW. GAIN INSIGHT—TAKE ACTION!)

1. Imagine that you are reading a classmate's essay and you realize that it is not his work. What clues would you see?

2. What does the word plagiarism mean? What are some potential consequences of plagiarism?

3. Is it possible to honestly submit the same paper for a grade in two different college courses? Explain.

4. Give some examples of how unintended plagiarism can occur. What might prevent it?

Dedicate Yourself to Honest Effort

Plagiarizing your work ultimately cheats your classmates, your instructors and you.

Are you willing to do what it takes to earn the best grades for your written assignments? Super. So are top students. Yet, some students are willing to risk cheating on their written submissions. Beware! It is a bad bet. Virtually any information students track down can be quickly located by most instructors. Therefore, pledge to avoid plagiarism at all costs.

What is plagiarism? **Plagiarism** occurs when students submit papers that contain some portion, if not all, of someone else's intellectual work and present it as their own. Taking advantage of another person's original ideas, findings or work without properly crediting its authorship is plagiarism.

Self-plagiarism results when students resubmit a legitimately written work from a previous class in a later course. Self-plagiarism also takes place when students submit the same paper in two classes, during the same semester, without the instructors' permission. When two instructors give permission, however, you can normally expect significantly more work, including additional reading, page count requirements, etc.

Unintended plagiarism is probably the most tragic of all. This occurs when students accidentally include someone else's words as their own. Sometimes, this is due to improperly placed quotation marks on a citation card. Less often, quotation marks may be entirely absent due to an improper transfer of information. Students who write particularly well may take such polished words as their own, resulting in unintended plagiarism.

Refer to your college's handbook for definitions of plagiarism and the penalties associated with it. Realize that the academic approach is to "trust but verify." The smart effort is an honest one.

"GENIUS BORROWS NOBLY." —RALPH WALDO EMERSON

Part 9

Create Outasight, Outrageous, On-Target Memory Solutions (That Will Have You High-Fiving Your Friends and Your Instructors Kissing Their Grade Books!!!)

Grade Grabber Exercise

(QUICKLY SCAN THIS EXERCISE. JOT DOWN IDEAS, IF YOU WISH. READ THE NEXT PAGE. WRITE OR ADD TO YOUR RESPONSES BELOW. GAIN INSIGHT—TAKE ACTION!)

1. How might rushing through your studies make it harder or easier to link new information with what you already know? Give an example.

2. In what kind of class is double-checking key details especially critical?

3. In what specific ways does interlocking what you learn increase your ability to think more effectively? Offer some examples.

4. Why do you think that personal commitment is a greater predictor of long-term academic success than curiosity? What words best capture the difference between commitment and curiosity?

Get a Lock on Content

Making connections is your master key
to a memorable learning experience.

Have you ever noticed that bright students seem to recall more course content with less effort? Would you like to take the shortest path to academic mastery? You can, if you are willing to take the time to **create connections between what you already know and what you need to learn.**

Consider the following **three-step approach** as a master key to expand your study ability and "get a lock" on course material:

1. **Link** new study content to what you already know.
2. **Lock** new learning into memory, but double-check key details first. False impressions hurt your grades.
3. **Interlock** this new learning with insights gained from your instructor, fellow classmates and study partners. Your interlocking knowledge base will sharpen your recall, questioning and critical-thinking skills.

If you link, lock and continually interlock what you learn, you will be better prepared to take part in class discussions and pass virtually any test. Even more important, you will quickly develop an almost uncanny ability to voice the kind of insights that will benefit your instructor, your classmates and you, as well.

Applying this simple three-step approach can provide one of the fastest paths to positive change, academic excellence and improved recall. This master key remains in your hands, and it is up to you to use it.

What is needed is genuine, deep-down commitment on your part. Nothing will happen unless you become passionate about your own stake in your future. Take action and apply these steps to your studies. Do you have the will to win? Why not take up your own challenge to do all you can do? Begin where you are and let your mind soar!

"EVEN THE WILDEST DREAMS HAVE TO START SOMEWHERE."
—OPRAH WINFREY

Grade Grabber Exercise

(QUICKLY SCAN THIS EXERCISE. JOT DOWN ADDITIONAL IDEAS, IF YOU WISH. READ THE NEXT PAGE. RETURN TO THE FOLLOWING SUGGESTIONS. GAIN INSIGHT—TAKE ACTION!)

1. Select one of the following descriptions to make one element of the **Garden of Eden** story notable, novel and fun. Picture your idea as part of a billboard ad campaign. Make it easy to recall.

GIGANTIC   **TINY**   **ABSURD**   **INCALCULABLE**

ENTERPRISING   **TIMID**   **UNINHIBITED**

ANGRY   **HAPPY**   **VULNERABLE**

MELTING   **SCARY**   **SLOPPY**

Take a Bite Out of Memorization

Garden variety substitutions
trigger much juicier recall.

There are times when the **simplest memory technique** is the best. Here is one. Many top students inject an inventive element into study content. It can make your own recall easier.

Jeff, an outstanding student, calls it the **"Garden of Eden" approach**. It occurred to him when he was studying botany.

> While studying plant classifications, I was surprised to learn that tomatoes are properly classified as fruits, not vegetables. Tomatoes are fruits? Every grocery list that I had seen included tomatoes with vegetables, never fruits. For some reason, this unexpected shift in classification made the **new concept** stick in my mind. Would it be possible **to consciously generate** similar mental shifts without relying on chance? The idea seemed promising. Suddenly, an insight flashed into my mind. A tomato is a fruit. Great! I pictured a ripe, red tomato. I asked myself, "What red-colored fruit looks most like a tomato?" An apple, of course! All I needed to do was to **imagine a memorable story** in which a tomato would replace an apple. Visualizing Eve taking a bite out of a tomato in the Garden of Eden made **the link** between tomatoes and apples clear and memorable.

Novelty is found in humor, surprise and absurdity. It can provide you with one of the most helpful and flexible ways to powerfully encode information. It is simple, fun and smart to be "crazy like a fox." After all, who cannot **visualize** a wild stallion making its own ketchup, if that is what it takes **to trigger recall**?

"THE MAN WHO CANNOT IMAGINE A HORSE GALLOPING ON A TOMATO IS AN IDIOT." —ANDRÉ BRETON

Grade Grabber Exercise

(QUICKLY SCAN THIS EXERCISE. JOT DOWN IDEAS, IF
YOU WISH. READ THE NEXT PAGE. WRITE OR ADD TO
YOUR RESPONSES BELOW. GAIN INSIGHT—TAKE ACTION!)

1. Recall several advertising rhymes that you regularly hear.
   What makes them so memorable to you? How might you
   apply what you have observed to your own studies?

2. Why is it important to be critical about what we encode in
   our minds? In what way might memory devices lead to wrong
   assumptions? Give several examples.

3. Why is a playful attitude often much more important than a
   hard-driving approach? Does suspending your judgment in
   creating novel rhymes mean that logic has no key role to play?
   Explain.

4. Top students often comment that once they have taken a
   creative leap during study, recall is nearly a foregone
   conclusion. Often this happens without needing to use the
   rhyme or story. Why do you think this is so?

Creative Leaps Can Strengthen Recall

Smartly combine data, novelty and humor.

As a child your brain thrived on rhyme, play and novelty:

> Hey diddle diddle,
> The cat and the fiddle,
> The cow jumped over the moon,
> The little dog laughed to see such sport,
> And the dish ran away with the spoon.

Top students often use rhyme and novelty to turn academic work into child's play. Assume, for example, that you are taking a chemistry lab course. **You need to remember to pour acid into water—never the other way around.** Why? The splash caused by water poured into an acid bath can result in a severe burn.

One top student devised a simple, easy-to-remember and effective rhyme to avoid that mistake:

> Do as you ought-er,
> Pour **acid into water**.

And how might you creatively remember information? **Adopt an open, innovative and playful attitude.** Imagine James, a student who is busily preparing for a test on the Russo-Japanese War. He is frustrated by his inability to recall that **The Battle of Tsushima** was won by **Admiral Togo**. Instinctively, James grabs pen and paper and writes **Tsushima** and **Togo** at the top of the page. After a few playful attempts, he notices the familiar word "sushi" in the spelling of Tsushima and circles it. He also circles "T," "ma," and "Togo." And an unforgettable memory story results:

> Order <u>T</u>-ea and <u>sushi</u> for your <u>ma</u> — "<u>To go</u>!"

"DON'T PLAY WHAT'S THERE. PLAY WHAT'S NOT THERE."
—MILES DAVIS

Use "Sound-Alike" Images to Recall Numbered Items

CREATING CONCRETE "SOUND-ALIKE" IMAGES FOR ABSTRACT NUMBERS ENCOURAGES EFFICIENT STUDY, ORGANIZATION AND POINT-BY-POINT RECALL OF KEY COURSE CONTENT.

Practice by using the following **sound-alike** number nicknames.

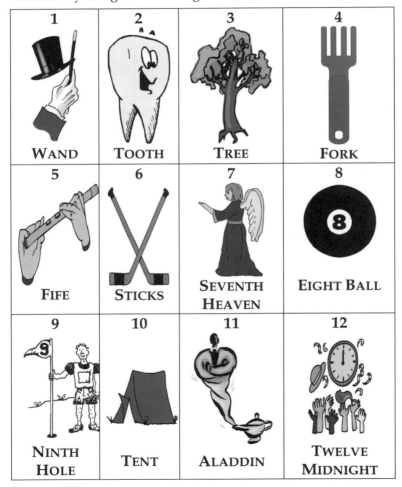

1	2	3	4
WAND	TOOTH	TREE	FORK
5	6	7	8
FIFE	STICKS	SEVENTH HEAVEN	EIGHT BALL
9	10	11	12
NINTH HOLE	TENT	ALADDIN	TWELVE MIDNIGHT

Put Teeth into Recall
Turn any numbered list into easy prey.

Would you like to recall information better than ever before? What if you could make key test information as vivid and easy to remember as outrageous tabloid-style headlines? You know the ones—"Toothy Venus Flytrap Eats Cow!" Almost all top students "eschew" the tabloids. Yet, many of them routinely use humor, novelty and vivid "sound-alike" target words to activate recall. You can, too!

Jill Johnson is not a genius, but she is able to recall more details than most students. She explains, "I always had trouble remembering numbered lists, in and out of order. I finally came up with a solution as I was attempting to learn the nine planets of our solar system: **1. Mercury; 2. Venus; 3. Earth; 4. Mars; 5. Jupiter; 6. Saturn; 7. Uranus; 8. Neptune; 9. Pluto.**

"Organizing **target information**, creating **sound-alike word pictures** for important material and merging numbers and content into funny-sounding but **memorable headlines** works. With a little planning you can make it easier to recall the order, number and names of any information that you need to remember."

SOUND-ALIKE	PLANET	MEMORABLE HEADLINE
1. = Wand	Mercury	Magic **Wand** grabbed by Greek god **Mercury** during relay!
2. = Tooth	Venus	**Toothy Venus** flytrap eats cow!
3. = Tree	Earth	**Tree** kicks **Earth** at picnickers!
4. = Fork	Mars	"**Fork**-only rule" **Mars** soup eating contest!
5. = Fife	Jupiter	**Fife** launches **Jupiter** rocket
6. = Sticks	Saturn	**Sticks** sighted in **Saturn**'s rings
7. = Seventh Heaven	Uranus	**Seventh Heaven** star tells fans "U-RAN-US" ragged!
8. = Eight Ball	Neptune	**Eight Ball** hits **Neptune** in head!
9. = Ninth Hole	Pluto	**Ninth Hole** flag stolen by **Pluto**!

"WHEN A THING IS FUNNY, SEARCH IT FOR A HIDDEN TRUTH."
–GEORGE BERNARD SHAW

Grade Grabber Exercise

(QUICKLY SCAN THIS EXERCISE. THE FIRST TWO IMAGES
ARE REPRESENTATIVE OF WHAT NUMBERS COULD LOOK
LIKE IF THEY BECAME VISUALS. READ THE NEXT PAGE.
CREATE YOUR OWN GRAPHICS FOR THE REMAINING NUMBERS!)

Resist the temptation to write words. Instead, try sketching ideas.

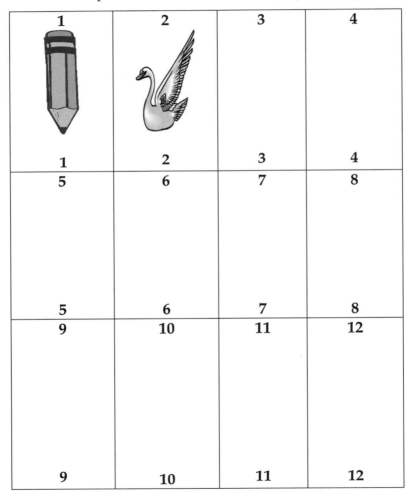

Morph Number Shapes into "Instant-on" Pictures

Visually organize content with number icon look-alikes.

They say that a picture is worth a thousand words. Studies show that students can **learn more by using** multiple sensory channels. To add variety to your studies, here is a novel idea for memorizing numbered lists, steps, etc. that relies solely on **your visual ability**.

Nathan is **an art major**. He **developed** a list of a dozen number stand-ins that can be used to create memorable links every bit as useful as the "sound-alike" number method. (See "Put Teeth into Recall.")

Nathan has always been a very visually minded person. As far back as he can remember, he has always been able to recall graphics faster than strictly verbal information. Nathan observes, "I like to add sketches to my lecture notes, not because I am bored, but because something just 'clicks' for me when I do."

How does this visual perception apply to numbers? Nathan discovered that when he squinted at numbers, he could more easily reimagine them as familiar shapes. Through curiosity, creativity and a couple of days to play with the idea, "1" became a pencil, "2" became a swan or a duck. And so it went. He explains, "I sketched **twelve specific items with shapes similar enough to numbers to** represent them as part of my memory system. You don't really need to be an artist to think like one," Nathan adds. "All you need is a visual memory for shapes. Memorizing can **make study into a game of perception**, rather than of hard work."

By **recasting each number form into a person, animal or thing,** Nathan **created** enough **at-a-glance objects to** satisfy his graphic intelligence and **easily organize** his **studies**.

For example, he was able **to memorize** French by picturing the shape of his lead pencil (one) and **repeat**ing <<un>> in his target language. He visualized a cartoon of a pencil putting unleaded gas (what else?) into his tank. A swan (two) in a pond heavy with dew was close enough to <<deux>> to **recall** that item. So it went.

"EVEN SILENCE SPEAKS." –HAUSA PROVERB

Grade Grabber Exercise

(REREAD "PUT TEETH INTO RECALL" AND "MORPH NUMBER SHAPES INTO 'INSTANT-ON' PICTURES." THOUGHTFULLY DO THE FOLLOWING EXERCISES!)

1. Refer to the "Morph Number Shapes" table. Create your own "tabloid-style" visuals by pairing numbers with the terms below. For example: Giant **Pencil** Attacks **Earth**; **Swan** Gone with **Wind**; **Key Ring** Sparks **Fire**; **Cactus** Flees **Water** Hole.

NUMBER + ENTRY	RECALL COMBO	NUMBER + ENTRY	RECALL COMBO
1 + EARTH	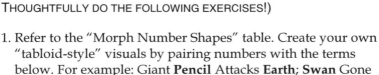	7 + BIG DIPPER	
2 + WIND		8 + MOON	
3 + FIRE		9 + COMET	
4 + WATER		10 + SUN	
5 + ATOM		11 + GAS	
6 + EINSTEIN		12 + RAYS	

Morph Numbers with the Following Shapes Table

MANY TOP STUDENTS MORPH NUMBERS INTO SHARP, TWIN-SHAPED MEMORY HOOKS. NUMBERED MEMORIZATION IS TRICKY. AT-A-GLANCE OBJECTS MAKE IT AUTOMATIC. USE INCREASES YOUR RECALL MASTERY.

Use your mind to morph each number as your fingertip traces it.

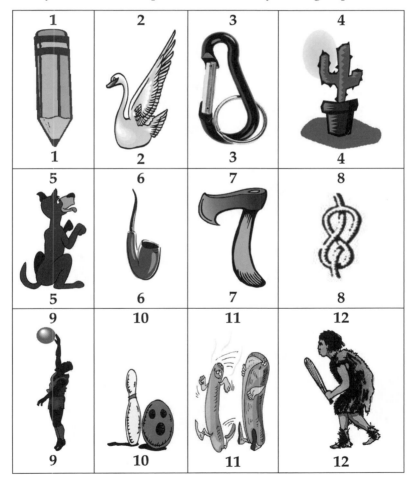

"SYMMETRY IS WHAT WE SEE AT A GLANCE." —BLAISE PASCAL

Grade Grabber Exercise

(QUICKLY SCAN THIS EXERCISE. JOT DOWN IDEAS, IF YOU WISH. READ THE NEXT PAGE. WRITE OR ADD TO YOUR RESPONSES BELOW. GAIN INSIGHT—TAKE ACTION!)

1. Adopt or adapt **sound-alike** images for all alphabet letters.

A	B	C	D
ABE	BEE	C VITAMIN	DEED
E	**F**	**G**	**H**
EAT	F (FULL)	G (RATED)	H (SIGN)
I	**J**	**K**	**L**
I-BEAM	JAYBIRD	KANGAROO	ELEVATOR
M	**N**	**O**	**P**
MEN	ENDZONE	OATS	PEAS

ABCs for Vivid Recall: Step I

A sound-alike image alphabet builds a better organized memory.

You automatically create mental associations about all sorts of information on a daily basis. Such natural spontaneity is good and helpful, but be careful of relying too heavily on basic memory skills. These will not serve you well in college. In order to **avoid hit-or-miss study approaches,** top students often **develop** tactics such as the **sound-alike image alphabet.** Forging both rhyme and reason into a powerful, organized memory tool is as easy as ABC.

Refer to the letter/picture table on the facing page. Each letter appears with **an image.** The name of each image **rhymes with the letter shown.** For example, "Abe" Lincoln appears in the same box as the letter "A," a picture of a "Bee" is found inside the box marked "B" and "C vitamin" tablets are seen under the letter "C."

Practice the sound-alike alphabet until it becomes automatic. Pronounce each letter, allowing its sound-alike image to appear in your mind's eye: Abe, Bee, C vitamin, Deed, Eat, etc. Should a particular letter not come to mind, simply look at the table and repeat the letter name. This will help you to fix the sound-alike image in your mind. Be patient with yourself.

With modest effort on your part, these sound-alike images can become permanent memory hooks **for organizing any study items you wish to remember.** (See "Put Teeth into Recall.")

Try these simple examples: Imagine Abe and a Mars space launch. As the rocket lifts off, see millions of Lincoln pennies falling on the launch pad. Really see it. Next, picture a bee at the controls of an old wood-burning locomotive, as you watch millions of bees pouring from the smokestack. Finally, imagine that your college library now looks like a giant C vitamin bottle.

Recite and visualize the sound-alike images: **A (Abe), B (bee), and C (C vitamin).** You should **remember each item by its letter "hook" and vice versa.** Locomotive was linked to which letter?

Grade Grabber Exercise

(QUICKLY SCAN THIS EXERCISE. JOT DOWN IDEAS, IF YOU WISH. READ THE NEXT PAGE. WRITE OR ADD TO YOUR RESPONSES BELOW. GAIN INSIGHT—TAKE ACTION!)

1. Adopt or adapt **sound-alike** images for all alphabet letters.

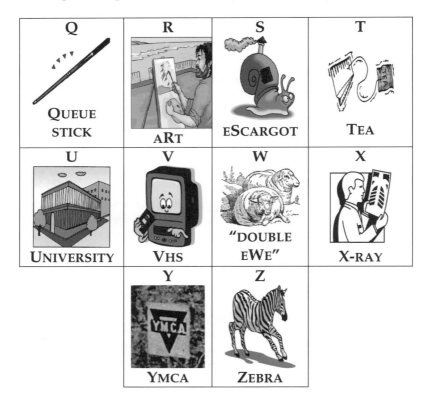

Q	R	S	T
QUEUE STICK	ART	eSCARGOT	TEA
U	V	W	X
UNIVERSITY	VHS	"DOUBLE eWe"	X-RAY
Y	Z		
YMCA	ZEBRA		

2. Once you have memorized your sound-alike alphabet, think about how you might apply it to lists of up to twenty-six entries, spreadsheet work, the Periodic Table of the Elements, Library of Congress numbers or any other important memory tasks. Top students are not perfect, just successful. Practice. Simplify. Make your path to college success "as easy as ABC."

ABCs for Vivid Recall: Step II

A sound-alike image alphabet builds a better organized memory.

Would you like to recall more information than you ever dreamed possible? Many former mediocre students have discovered that with modest practice, they can outperform most of their classmates and top grade earners, as well. **Building on what you have already learned and applying it to the remaining sound-alike letters, Q through Z, will give you incredible benefits.** If you have taken the time to fully master all of the exercises to this point, you will find committing these last letters to memory easy to do. If you have not already done so, be sure to go back and read, practice and apply "Put Teeth into Recall" and "ABCs for Vivid Recall: Step I" first.

You have already been shown how the ABCs of recall can be used as simple memory hooks (Abe + Mars space launch, etc.). Now you are ready to **combine the sound-alike alphabet with the sound-alike number system** that you learned earlier. A parking lot number provides a practical way for you to easily practice this type of recall.

Imagine that you have just entered the campus parking lot. After looking for what seems an eternity, you finally locate a **parking space marked "T-871."** Using the sound-alike alphabet and the sound-alike number systems, you are able to create an outrageous image story to lock that number into your memory.

Since **sound-alike letter "T" is pictured as a Tea bag**, you imagine parking a giant tea bag. Now use **sound-alike number images to remember 871.** For example, imagine a tire so over inflated that an **(8) eight ball-**sized bubble appears. Suddenly, an angel appears from **(7) seventh heaven** waving a magic **(1) wand.**

It only takes a few seconds to create these stories. Always be sure to repeat them several times from memory so that you will be able to easily recall each detail. Use all of your senses. Replaying your story as vividly as possible helps to ensure proper encoding.

"OUT OF SIGHT, OUT OF MIND." —LADY ANNE BACON

MY DAILY AGENDA

DATE-

ITEM	√	PLANNED TASK
1		
2		
3		
4		
5		
6		
7		
8		
9		
10		

QUARTER HOUR STUDY POWER

DATE-
SUBJECT-
TEXT-

(Complete this form* using the instructions on pages 38 and 39.
Feel free to use graph paper if you prefer. Do what works best!)

TIME: START TO FINISH	15	30	45	00	ACTUAL HOURLY STUDY TIME	ACTUAL HOURLY PAGES READ	ASSIGNED PAGES:
					TOTAL STUDY TIME	TOTAL PAGES READ	ASSIGNED PAGES REMAINING

www.gradegrabbers.com

QUARTER HOUR STUDY POWER

DATE-
SUBJECT-
TEXT-

(Complete this form* using the instructions on pages 38 and 39.
You have a lot to read. Why not copy a stack of these two pages?

TIME: START TO FINISH	15	30	45	00	ACTUAL HOURLY STUDY TIME	ACTUAL HOURLY PAGES READ	ASSIGNED PAGES:
					TOTAL STUDY TIME	TOTAL PAGES READ	ASSIGNED PAGES REMAINING

BIBLIOGRAPHY FILE

AUTHOR-

TITLE-

[   ]

CITY: PUBLISHER, DATE-

LIBRARY & LOCATION	CALL NUMBER

RATE THIS TITLE: 1   2   3   4   5

COMMENTS-

ASK!!! YOU MAY BE CLOSER TO A BREAKTHROUGH THAN YOU REALIZE.
YOUR RESEARCH LIBRARIAN KNOWS HOW TO GET YOU THERE—FAST!

www.gradegrabbers.com

Index